# simply grilling

*105 recipes* for quick and casual grilling

by Jennifer Chandler

*with photography by* Justin Fox Burks

THOMAS NELSON
*Since 1798*

NASHVILLE   DALLAS   MEXICO CITY   RIO DE JANEIRO

# Other Books by Jennifer Chandler

*Simply Suppers*

*Simply Salads*

Published in Nashville, Tennessee, by Thomas Nelson. Thomas Nelson is a registered trademark of Thomas Nelson, Inc.

Photography by Justin Fox Burks

Thomas Nelson, Inc., titles may be purchased in bulk for educational, business, fund-raising, or sales promotional use. For information, please e-mail SpecialMarkets@ThomasNelson.com.

**Library of Congress Cataloging-in-Publication Data**

Chandler, Jennifer, 1970–
  Simply grilling : 105 recipes for quick and casual grilling / Jennifer Chandler ; with photography by Justin Fox Burks.
     p. cm.
  ISBN 978-1-4016-0451-6 (hardback)
  1. Barbecuing. 2. Cookbooks. I. Title.
  TX840.B3C475 2012
  641.7'6—dc23                                             2011042828

*Printed in the United States of America*

12 13 14 15 QGT 6 5 4 3 2 1

To Paul,
Hannah, and Sarah,
who make life
so delicious!

# Contents

# Introduction

Firing up the grill makes every meal with family and friends feel like a celebration.

Fragrant smoke wafting from the fire, juicy steaks sizzling on the grill, friends gathered on the back porch while the cook tends the grill . . . there is just something magical, fun, even primal about meals cooked outdoors over a hot grill.

I have to admit it. I used to be intimidated by the grill.

My childhood memories of grilling involve monstrous grills and smokers used in barbecue contests. When someone hosted a backyard barbecue, it meant they had been out there for hours stoking the fire to have the perfect slow and low flame for crafting smoky, fall-off-the-bone pork and chicken.

That type of "long and slow" grilling works well on weekends, but it is just not practical for weeknight meals.

The backyard barbecue I want to share with you is much more than just burgers and slow-cooked meats. It's easy, no-fuss grilling. It's quick-cooking items that you can dress up with a simple sauce or marinade. Recipes like Grilled Tomato and Vidalia Onion Bruschetta (page 33), Cedar Plank Salmon with Caper Remoulade (page 107), Chile-Rubbed Strip Steak with Lime-Chipotle Sauce (page 99), and Grilled Corn and Green Bean Salad (page 151) that will inspire you to light up your grill, even on the busiest night of the week.

Grilling is deliciously simple. It's the ideal cooking technique for a wide array of items such as meats, poultry, fish, steaks, vegetables, and even pizzas.

In *Simply Grilling*, I have compiled my favorite recipes for creating delicious dishes hot off the grill. Versatile dishes—mouthwatering appetizers and entrées, flame-kissed sides and salads, and decadent desserts—offer all the flavor and flair of crowd-pleasing fare without any of the fuss.

And as an added bonus, cleanup after grilling is a lot easier than a dinner that involves breaking out all the pots and pans (and washing them)!

So get out of the kitchen and fire up the grill!

# Grilling 101

## Grill Types

There are two main types of outdoor grills: gas and charcoal.

Each has its advantages and disadvantages, but what they both do is cook food on a rack above a heat source.

For everyday cooking, I prefer the convenience and consistency of a gas grill. It can be lit in seconds and the temperature set with the twist of a knob. And with no hot coals to worry about, cleanup is a breeze. Turning on a gas grill is just as simple as turning on the oven!

Charcoal tends to burn hotter than gas, allowing for a better sear and more of that wonderful smoky flavor that you can only get from cooking over wood or charcoal, but lighting a charcoal grill does require more time and energy than lighting a gas grill.

Basically, there is no right or wrong answer. Use whichever grill works best for you.

## Indoor Grilling

You can grill indoors? Yes!

Not everybody has a backyard or a grill. And even if you do have a grill, cold and rain can put a damper on outdoor cooking. A stove-top grill pan is the solution.

Cast-iron grill pans are my preference. They evenly distribute and retain the heat and can withstand high temperatures—key elements to giving your food that tasty char that mimics outdoor grilling. Nonstick grill pans have a nonstick coating that can be damaged when heated at high temperatures.

To know which of my recipes can be made indoors, look for the grill pan icon.

> **Tip:** *A blazing hot grill pan gets hot all over, including the handle. It's easy to forget this, and you can get badly burned. I angle the handle away from the heat and cover it with a pot holder as a reminder that the handle is hot.*

## Control the Heat

Most gas grills come with a thermometer or gauge to help you control the heat.

For gas grills without a thermometer or for charcoal grills, you can easily gauge the heat by simply holding your hand about 3 to 4 inches above the grates and counting the number of seconds you can stand the heat.

| Temperature | Thermometer | Hand Check |
| --- | --- | --- |
| High | 400°F to 450°F | for 1 to 2 seconds |
| Medium-High | 375°F to 400°F | for 2 to 3 seconds |
| Medium | 350°F to 375°F | for 3 to 4 seconds |
| Medium-Low | 325°F to 350°F | for 4 to 5 seconds |
| Low | 300°F to 325°F | for 5 seconds or more |

When using a gas grill, you can control the heat by simply turning the temperature knob.

When using a charcoal grill, you can control the heat two ways. First, move the coals. If the fire is burning too hot, reduce the heat by spreading out the coals. If it is too low, increase the heat by pushing the hot coals closer together and adding more charcoal to the outer edges. Second, use the vents to fine-tune your grill temperature. To raise the temperature, open the vents to allow more oxygen to fuel the fire. To lower the temperature, close the vents.

## Grilling Methods

While grills come in many shapes and sizes, there are only two methods for cooking on a grill: direct heat and indirect heat.

**Direct grilling** is the method of placing the food on the grill rack directly over the heat source. This method is best for searing and cooking small, tender cuts that cook in 30 minutes or less, such as steaks, burgers, boneless chicken, and vegetables.

**Indirect grilling** is the method of placing food on the grill rack away from or to the side of the heat source with the grill lid closed. This type of grilling cooks the food similar to roasting in an oven. This low and slow grilling method is best for cooking larger foods that take longer to cook.

For indirect grilling on a gas grill, just turn off one or more of the heating elements after preheating. To set up a charcoal grill for indirect grilling, place the hot coals on one side of the grill. A drip tray (a disposable foil pan) is placed below the food to prevent flare-ups from dripping juices and fats.

Since this book is about easily getting dinner on the table, most recipes in *Simply Grilling* will be cooked using the direct grilling method. The recipes that use indirect grilling methods have more detailed cooking instructions.

**Tip:** *If you find that your fire is too hot or your food is burning before it is done, you can set up your grill for both indirect and direct cooking. Sear foods first over direct heat and then move them to an area with no heat to finish cooking by indirect heat. This two-zone grilling is especially helpful for cooking foods like bone-in chicken.*

## Checking for Doneness

The best way to tell if a piece of meat is done is to use an instant-read thermometer. I'd be lost without mine.

Insert the thermometer into the center or thickest part of the meat, poultry, or fish to get the internal temperature. Make sure the tip of the thermometer doesn't touch any bone.

| | |
|---|---|
| Poultry | 165°F |
| Pork | 160°F |
| Beef: Rare | 125°F to 130°F |
| Beef: Medium-Rare | 130°F to 135°F |
| Beef: Medium | 140°F to 145°F |
| Beef: Well-Done | 160°F and higher |
| Fish | 145°F |

The USDA recommends that ground beef be cooked to an internal temperature of at least 160°F and steaks be cooked to at least 145°F.

I suggest taking the meat off the grill a few degrees below the desired temperature is reached. Ideally, you should always let your meat rest for about 5 minutes before slicing to allow the juices to evenly distribute. During this time, the meat will continue to cook, bringing it up to the desired temperature.

If you don't have a meat thermometer, you can use the "touch" test. As meat cooks, it gets firmer to the touch. Rare is really spongy and soft (like the flesh between your thumb and index finger when you pinch them together), medium is springy (like the flesh between your thumb and ring finger when you pinch them together), and well-done feels very firm.

A third way to test poultry and pork is to insert a skewer into the thickest part of the meat. If the juices run clear, the meat is cooked. If the juices are bloody, return the meat to the grill and continue cooking.

Fish should be cooked until it is opaque and flakes easily with a fork.

## Dress Up Your Grilled Dishes: Marinades, Rubs, Sauces, and Salsas

**Marinades 101:** Soaking your grill-bound meats in a delicious, aromatic marinade will add flavor and tenderness.

- Rinse all meats and vegetables and pat them dry with a paper towel before marinating.
- Choose a shallow, nonreactive dish just large enough to hold the meat in a single layer. Avoid metal containers because they may impart an unpleasant metallic taste to marinated foods.
- Be sure to turn the meat in order to coat the marinade on all sides.
- Chicken, pork, and tougher cuts of beef can marinate up to overnight. Smaller cuts of beef and lamb require only 2 to 4 hours. Fish and shellfish should not be marinated longer than an hour. For best results, always follow a recipe's suggested marinating times.

**Rubs 101:** Slathering meats with savory blends of herbs and spices transforms an ordinary piece of meat into a masterpiece.

- Homemade dry rubs can be made in advance. Keep them for several weeks, tightly sealed, in your spice cabinet.
- Lightly brushing the meat with olive oil or mustard before adding the dry rub will help the dry rub adhere to the meat.
- Use your fingers when adding a dry rub. Spread the rub evenly over the meat and press slightly to make it adhere.
- When making a dry rub, be sure all the ingredients are evenly mixed.

**Sauces 101:** Sensational sauces add a boost of flavor at the end of grilling.

- Most sauces can be made a day or two in advance. Cover and refrigerate them until you're ready to use them.
- Slather thick sauces on with a silicone or natural-bristle basting brush at the end of cooking.

*Resealable plastic bags are also great for marinating because you don't have to dirty a dish.*

- Sugar-based barbecue sauces should only be applied toward the end of cooking time since they burn easily.
- Oil-and-vinegar, citrus, and yogurt-based bastes and sauces can be brushed on the meat throughout the cooking time.

**Salsas 101:** Dress up your grilled dishes with a flavorful salsa.

- Most salsas can be made in advance. Store them covered in your refrigerator until you are ready to serve them.
- Salsas can be sweet or savory. Experiment with your favorite fruits and veggies.
- Fresh herbs tend to blacken when cut. Wait until just before serving to add fresh herbs to your salsas.

**Tip:** *To prevent bruising delicate fresh herbs when cutting, snip them with a sharp pair of scissors instead of using a knife. It is super easy, and there's no cutting board to wash!*

## Essential Grill Gear

**Chimney starter:** A must-have for charcoal grills. These metal cylinders are a safe, efficient, and environmentally friendly way to start a fire without charcoal fluid.

**Heavy-duty grill brush:** For best results, you need a clean grill. Scrub the grates while they are still warm.

**Meat thermometer:** An instant-read thermometer is the most reliable way to ensure food is cooked properly (see page 2 for a temperature guide).

**Tongs:** Metal tongs are the most frequently used cooking tool in my kitchen. I prefer the regular stainless-steel, spring-hinged tongs rather than the long handled tongs found in the barbecue section of the housewares store.

**Metal spatulas:** Because they are ideal for turning food, I recommend having both a long-handled, sturdy spatula as well as a wider-based fish spatula.

**Brushes:** Use for applying glazes, sauces, and oiling the grill grates. You can use either natural or silicone brushes. I prefer the natural brushes for glazes and thinner sauces and the silicone ones for thicker barbecue sauces.

**Grill basket or grill screen:** These inexpensive gadgets will keep small items from falling through the grates.

**Cast-iron pans and Dutch ovens:** Cast-iron cookware heats evenly and can withstand the high heat of the grill. Use them for simmering sauces and cooking sides right on the grill.

**Metal or bamboo skewers:** These are essential for kebabs and satays. If you are using bamboo skewers, be sure to soak them in water for at least 30 minutes to prevent burning the wood.

**Heat-resistant gloves or long oven mitts:** Protect your hands and forearms from a hot grill.

**Grill cover:** Keep your grill clean and rust-free by covering it with an inexpensive grill cover when the grill is not in use. Make sure your grill is cool before covering it.

## Bamboo Skewers 101

Ideally, bamboo skewers should be soaked in water for at least 30 minutes to prevent them from burning. If you are short on time or forgot to prep your skewers, a quick fix is to wrap the tips of the skewers in foil.

## 5 Tips to Master Grilling Meats

**Keep the grate hot, clean, and oiled:** A clean grill with oiled grates will keep food from sticking. Before placing food on a hot grill, scrub the grates with a heavy-duty grill brush, lightly brush the grates with oil using a brush or a paper towel, and scrub the grates one last time when you are finished cooking.

**Turn just once:** To get killer grill marks, turn the meat or veggies only after they have been on the grill for a couple of minutes. The meat is ready to be turned when it easily releases from the grill.

**Grip, don't stab:** Use a set of tongs, not a barbecue fork, to turn a piece of meat. Forks poke holes in meat, allowing those precious juices to drain out.

**Know when it's done:** Nothing is worse than an overcooked piece of meat. It is always better to err on the side of undercooking rather than overcooking. You can always put a piece of food back on the grill, but you can't salvage an overcooked dish. See page 4 for a detailed guide on checking doneness.

**Let it rest:** Allowing a piece of meat to rest for 5 minutes before slicing will give it time for the juices to recirculate, resulting in a more tender, juicy dish.

## Oil Your Grates

Oiling your grill grates creates a non-stick surface. I often use a brush with natural bristles to oil my grates. Another trick is to dip a paper towel or half an onion in vegetable oil and then use a pair of tongs to wipe the oil onto the clean, hot grill.

## Food Safety

• If you are marinating something for an hour or less, then it should be fine to leave it out in a cool place, but when in doubt, refrigerate it. Do not set a dish out to marinate in the hot sun.

• If marinating overnight, pull the dish out 30 minutes before cooking to allow it to come to room temperature. If you stick a cold dense piece of meat on a hot grill, you risk drying out the exterior of the meat before you've given the inside a chance to cook through.

- Marinades and sauces that have come in contact with raw meat should not be used on cooked meats. Either discard the marinade or bring it to a boil for 2 minutes before using it on cooked dishes. When I know that I would like to brush a finished dish with additional marinade or sauce, I reserve some marinade in a separate container when I make it.
- Remove excess fats and marinades from foods to reduce flare-ups.
- Always make sure chicken and pork are thoroughly cooked before eating it.
- Do not return cooked foods to the unwashed platter or plate that held raw food.

## Tips

Have you ever read a recipe and wondered if you could do a portion of the work ahead of time or substitute an ingredient in your pantry for a more exotic ingredient? I tried to think of all the different tips and variations that I wished the cookbooks on my shelves offered. Here are the six basic tips you will find throughout *Simply Grilling*. I hope they help.

 **Cooking Tips:** Detailed information on cooking techniques, substitutes, and "food facts" about the dishes and specific ingredients.

**Do-Ahead:** Tips and strategies to take the stress out of dinnertime.

 **Variations:** Tips on how to put a unique spin on a dish.

 **Marinate:** To help you plan, I let you know at a glance how long a dish needs to marinate.

 **Suggested Sides:** Tips to help you plan your menu.

 **Grill Pan:** Too rainy or cold to grill? Don't own an outdoor grill? This icon lets you knows which dishes can easily be made indoors on a grill pan.

# Starters

I think some of the best meals I have ever had have been at home.

Don't get me wrong, I love to eat out. It's fun to let someone else do the cooking and cleaning while I just sit back and enjoy the meal. Also, dining at restaurants is where I get some of my best inspiration for recipes to create.

But most of my best dining memories have been sitting around the dinner table with goods friends and family.

Having guests for dinner for me is a casual affair. My attitude is always "the more, the merrier." Chairs from every room in the house are squeezed around the table. Kids are often relegated to a picnic blanket set out in the yard (or in the winter on my den floor!).

I also love to have my friends with me while I cook. It's more fun for all if my guests take part in the action. I invited them over so I can spend time with them—not have them in another room while I'm in the kitchen!

I always have an appetizer on the table for us to enjoy while dinner is finishing up on the grill. Easy yet impressive starters hot off the grill—like Grilled Artichokes (page 23), Grilled Pizzas (page 29), and Grilled Salmon Dip (page 31)—keep everyone happy while we chat, sip on a refreshing beverage, and keep one eye on the grill.

# Bacon-Wrapped Dates

*Whoever came up with the combination of supersweet dates with smoky bacon is a genius in my book. I always plan to make extra because I can't help but taste-test a few!*

Vegetable oil, for the grates
1 pound (12 to 13 slices) bacon, preferably
    thick-cut
25 Medjool dates (about 3/4 pound)

Toothpicks (soaked in water for 30
    minutes)

▶ Preheat a clean grill to medium-high with the lid closed for 8 to 10 minutes. Lightly brush the grates with oil.

▶ Cut the bacon slices in half. Set aside.

▶ Remove the pits from the dates by cutting the tips off each end of the dates and inserting the flat end of a skewer until it pushes the pit out of the date.

▶ Wrap each date with a slice of bacon and secure with a toothpick.

▶ Place the dates on the grill. Close the lid and cook until the bacon is brown and crispy, about 3 to 4 minutes per side.

Serves 8 to 10.

 **Do-Ahead:** The dates can be prepped up to 6 hours ahead. Cover and refrigerate until ready to grill.

**Variation:** You could stuff the dates with a little blue cheese for an added zing.

# Buffalo Sliders with Blue Cheese Slaw

*Burgers meet Buffalo Chicken Wings! What better combination for a game-day appetizer?!*

1/4 cup buffalo hot sauce
1/4 cup mayonnaise
2 cups shredded coleslaw mix (or finely shredded green cabbage)
1/2 cup blue cheese dressing
1/4 cup crumbled blue cheese

Kosher salt and freshly ground black pepper
1 1/2 pounds ground beef chuck or sirloin
Vegetable oil, for the grates
8 mini-hamburger rolls, split in half

▸ In small bowl whisk together the hot sauce and mayonnaise. Cover and refrigerate until ready to serve.

▸ Place the slaw in a medium bowl. Add the blue cheese dressing and crumbled blue cheese. Toss until evenly coated. Season with the salt and pepper to taste. Refrigerate until ready to serve.

▸ Place the ground beef in a large bowl. Generously season with salt and pepper. Divide the meat into 8 equal portions. Being careful not to overwork or compact the meat too much, pat each portion into a 3/4-inch thick patty.

▸ Preheat a clean grill to medium-high with the lid closed for 8 to 10 minutes. Lightly brush the grates with oil.

▸ Place the burgers on the grill. Close the lid and cook, turning once, until the desired temperature is reached, 4 to 5 minutes per side for medium. About 1 minute before the burgers are done, place the buns, cut-side down, on the grill and cook until lightly toasted.

▸ To serve, spoon the buffalo mayonnaise on the bottom half of the buns. Place the burgers on each bottom half, and top each burger with a spoonful of the blue cheese slaw and the bun tops. Serve warm.

Serves 6.

**V** **Variation:** For a leaner burger, substitute ground turkey for the ground beef. Since turkey is so lean, be sure to use ground turkey that is at least 7 percent fat. Using anything leaner will result in dry burgers. I also recommend adding 1/4 cup Panko bread crumbs to help the ground turkey hold together better on the grill.

**Cooking Tip:** You can always use a bottled blue cheese dressing, but it is really easy to make a homemade version. See page 35 for my recipe.

# Caribbean Grilled Shrimp with Pineapple Salsa

*I like to grill shrimp on skewers so I don't lose any between the grates, but you can use a grill basket if you prefer.*

### For the Pineapple Salsa:
2 cups diced fresh pineapple
1/4 cup finely diced red onions (half a small onion)
1 tablespoon seeded and finely diced fresh jalapenos
1 tablespoon freshly grated lime zest
3 tablespoons freshly squeezed lime juice
Kosher salt and freshly ground black pepper
2 tablespoons coarsely chopped fresh cilantro

### For the Caribbean Grilled Shrimp:
1/2 cup coarsely chopped fresh cilantro
1/2 cup coarsely chopped scallions
1 tablespoon diced green chiles
2 cloves garlic, finely minced
2 tablespoons freshly squeezed lime juice
2 tablespoons olive oil
2 teaspoons ground cumin
3 pounds medium-large shrimp (16-20 count)
Vegetable oil, for the grates
Skewers (if using bamboo, soak in water for 30 minutes)

▸ To make the Pineapple Salsa: In a large mixing bowl combine the pineapple, red onions, jalapenos, lime zest, and lime juice. Season with the salt and pepper to taste. Add the cilantro and gently toss to combine. Cover and refrigerate until ready to serve.

▸ To make the Caribbean Grilled Shrimp: In a blender or food processor, puree the cilantro, scallions, green chiles, garlic, lime juice, olive oil, and cumin.

▸ Peel and devein the shrimp, leaving the tail attached. Place the shrimp in a large bowl and toss with the marinade. Cover and refrigerate for at least 30 minutes or up to 1 hour. Remove the shrimp from the marinade, drain off any excess, and discard the marinade.

▸ Preheat a clean grill to medium-high with the lid closed for 8 to 10 minutes. Lightly brush the grates with oil.

▸ Thread the shrimp on skewers. Place on the grill. Close the lid and cook, turning once, until they turn pink, 2 to 3 minutes per side. Serve with a generous spoonful of the Pineapple Salsa.

Serves 4 to 6.

**Cooking Tips:** Do not overcook the shrimp, or they will be chewy. When they are pink, they are done. To save time, you can purchase fresh or frozen shrimp that have already been peeled and deveined. Fresh pineapple is best, but canned pineapple can be used instead.

**Do-Ahead:** The Pineapple Salsa can be made 4 hours ahead. Store covered in the refrigerator until ready to serve.

**Marinate:** 30 minutes or up to 1 hour.

# Charred Corn and Black Bean Salsa

*I love the smoky flavor that grilled corn gives to this Tex-Mex salsa. Serve it as an appetizer with chips, as a side dish, or as a garnish for chicken and fish.*

Vegetable oil, for the grates
4 large ears fresh corn, shucked
2 tablespoons unsalted butter, softened
Kosher salt and freshly ground black pepper
1 can (15-ounce) black beans, rinsed and drained
1/4 cup finely diced red bell pepper (half a small pepper)

1/4 cup finely diced green bell peppers (half a small pepper)
1/4 cup finely diced red onions (half a small onion)
2 tablespoons finely chopped fresh cilantro
1 tablespoon extra virgin olive oil
1 teaspoon red wine vinegar
1/4 teaspoon cayenne pepper

▶ Preheat a clean grill to medium-high with the lid closed for 8 to 10 minutes. Lightly brush the grates with oil.

▶ Brush the corn evenly with the butter. Season with the salt and pepper to taste.

▶ Place the corn on the grill. Close the lid and cook, turning occasionally, until just tender and slightly charred on all sides, 8 to 10 minutes total. Transfer the corn to a cutting board to cool.

▶ When the corn is cool enough to handle, use a sharp knife to carefully slice the kernels off the cob. Discard the cob. Place the kernels in a large bowl. Add the beans, red peppers, green peppers, onions, cilantro, olive oil, vinegar, and cayenne pepper. Gently toss to combine. Season with salt and pepper to taste.

▶ Serve chilled.

Serves 6.

 **Do-Ahead:** This salsa can be made up to 1 day in advance. Cover and refrigerate until ready to serve. If making the salsa more than an hour in advance, I recommend chopping and adding the cilantro just before serving. Delicate herbs like cilantro and basil tend to blacken when cut too far in advance.

# Chicken Satays with Peanut Dipping Sauce

*For parties, satays are a great idea because they are simple to prepare yet make a dramatic presentation. Plus, I don't think I have ever found a food on a stick I didn't love!*

## For the Chicken Satays:

- 1/4 cup toasted sesame oil
- 3 tablespoons soy sauce
- 2 cloves garlic, minced
- 1 tablespoon finely grated fresh ginger
- 1/2 teaspoon crushed red pepper flakes
- 4 skinless, boneless chicken breasts (about 1 1/2 pounds), cut into strips
- Vegetable oil, for the grates
- Kosher salt and freshly ground black pepper
- Skewers (if using bamboo, soak in water for 30 minutes)

## For the Peanut Dipping Sauce:

- 1/4 cup rice wine vinegar
- 2 tablespoons creamy peanut butter
- 1 teaspoon finely grated fresh ginger
- 1 tablespoon soy sauce
- 1 tablespoon honey
- 2 teaspoons toasted sesame oil
- 1/2 cup canola oil
- A pinch of crushed red pepper flakes (optional)
- Kosher salt and freshly ground black pepper
- 1/4 cup chopped peanuts, for garnish

▶ To prepare the Chicken Satays: In a shallow nonreactive dish just large enough to hold the chicken in a single layer, combine the sesame oil, soy sauce, garlic, ginger, and red pepper flakes. Place the chicken strips in the marinade and gently toss until well coated. Cover, place in the refrigerator, and marinate for at least 20 minutes but not more than an hour.

▶ To make the Peanut Dipping Sauce: In a small bowl whisk together the vinegar, peanut butter, ginger, soy sauce, honey, sesame oil, canola oil, and red pepper flakes. Season with the salt and pepper to taste.

▶ Pour the sauce into a serving bowl and garnish with the chopped peanuts. Cover and refrigerate until ready to use.

▶ To finish the Chicken Satays: Preheat a clean grill to medium-high with the lid closed for 8 to 10 minutes. Lightly brush the grates with oil.

▶ Generously season the chicken with salt and pepper. Thread each chicken strip lengthwise onto a skewer.

▶ Place the chicken on the grill. Close the lid and cook, turning once, until no longer pink in the middle, about 3 to 5 minutes on each side. Serve the satays with the peanut sauce on the side.

Serves 8.

**Do-Ahead:** The peanut sauce can be made up to 2 days in advance. Store covered in the refrigerator.

**Variation:** This recipe is equally delicious when made with flank steak.

**Marinate:** 20 minutes. Not more than 1 hour.

# Grilled Artichokes with Lemony Dipping Sauce

*Everything from the kitchen of my friend Lucia Heros is absolutely delicious, and this grilled veggie appetizer is no exception. The balsamic marinade is what makes this version deliciously unique.*

### For the Grilled Artichokes:

1 lemon
4 large artichokes (3 to 3 1/2 pounds total)
1/4 cup balsamic vinegar
1/4 cup olive oil
1 tablespoon dried Italian seasoning
1 teaspoon garlic salt
Kosher salt and freshly ground black pepper
Vegetable oil, for the grates

### For the Lemony Dipping Sauce:

1/4 cup mayonnaise
2/3 cup olive oil
2 tablespoons Dijon mustard
1/4 cup freshly squeezed lemon juice
1 tablespoon dried Italian seasoning
2 cloves garlic, minced
Kosher salt and freshly ground black pepper

▶ To make the Grilled Artichokes: Fill a large pot with cold water and add the juice of 1 lemon. Trim an inch off the bottom of each artichoke stem and place the whole artichoke in the water.

▶ When all the artichokes are prepared, cover the pan and bring to a boil. Boil until the base of the stem is tender and can be easily pierced with a fork, about 20 minutes. Transfer the artichokes to a cutting board and let rest until cool enough to handle, about 15 minutes.

▶ Slice the artichokes in half lengthwise. Scoop out the choke and first few inner layers in the center until the bottom is revealed. Place the prepared artichokes on a rimmed baking sheet cut-side up.

▶ In a small bowl, whisk together the balsamic vinegar, olive oil, Italian seasoning, and garlic salt. Pour the mixture over the artichokes. Season with the salt and pepper to taste. Allow the artichokes to marinate for 15 to 20 minutes, while preparing the dipping sauce and preheating the grill.

▶ To make the Lemony Dipping Sauce: In a medium bowl, combine the mayonnaise, olive oil, Dijon mustard, lemon juice, Italian seasoning, and garlic. Season to taste with the salt and pepper. Cover and refrigerate until ready to serve.

▶ To finish the Grilled Artichokes: Preheat a clean grill to medium-high with the lid closed for 8 to 10 minutes. Lightly brush the grates with oil.

▶ Place the artichokes on the grill, cut-side down, and close the lid. Cook, turning once, until tender and lightly charred, about 5 to 8 minutes per side. Transfer to a serving platter and serve with the dipping sauce.

Serves 4 to 6.

**Cooking Tip:** I love the flavor that Lucia's balsamic marinade gives this dish. But for a simpler flavor, skip the marinade and simply brush the par-cooked artichokes with olive oil prior to grilling and then squeeze fresh lemon juice over the top of the finished dish.

 **Marinate:** 15 to 20 minutes.

# Grilled Nachos

*Grilled nachos make a fun outdoor appetizer. My cast-iron fajita pan takes them from the grill to the table.*

1 bag (13-ounce) tortilla chips
1 cup shredded Monterey jack cheese, divided
1 cup shredded Cheddar cheese, divided
1 can (15-ounce) black beans, rinsed and drained, divided
1/4 cup thinly sliced scallions, divided

1/4 cup sliced jalapenos (pickled or fresh), divided
2 cloves garlic, minced, divided
1 tablespoon ground cumin, divided
1/2 cup diced plum tomatoes
2 tablespoons finely chopped fresh cilantro
1/2 cup sour cream (optional garnish)

▶ Preheat a clean grill to medium-high with the lid closed for 8 to 10 minutes.

▶ Place a single layer of chips on a cast-iron pan or a grill tray and top with 1/3 of the cheeses, black beans, scallions, jalapenos, garlic, and cumin. Repeat to make 2 more layers.

▶ Place the tray in the center of the grill. Close the lid and cook until the cheese is melted, 8 to 10 minutes. Remove the tray from the grill and sprinkle the tomatoes and cilantro over the top. Serve immediately, garnished with sour cream if desired.

Serves 8.

**Cooking Tip:** If you're going on a picnic, assemble the nachos at home in a disposable foil pan. You can grill and serve from that same pan.

**Variation:** For a heartier nacho, add sautéed chorizo sausage or roasted chicken.

# Grilled Peaches with Balsamic Syrup and Crumbled Blue Cheese

*A sweet and savory marriage made in heaven. The balsamic syrup is what makes this dish a knockout. The simple process of reducing an everyday balsamic vinegar concentrates the flavor and richness, making a lovely syrup that is both sweet and tart.*

1 cup balsamic vinegar
Vegetable oil, for the grates
6 peaches, halved and pitted
2 tablespoons canola oil

1/2 cup crumbled blue cheese
1/4 cup chopped fresh basil

▶ Place the balsamic vinegar in a small saucepan. Bring to a boil over medium-high heat. Reduce the temperature to medium, and simmer until the liquid is reduced by half and becomes syrupy, about 10 minutes. Set aside.

▶ Preheat a clean grill to medium with the lid closed for 8 to 10 minutes. Lightly brush the grates with vegetable oil.

▶ Brush the cut sides of each peach half with the canola oil.

▶ Place the peaches on the grill, cut-side down. Close the lid and cook until grill marks appear, about 3 minutes. Turn and cook until the peaches soften and just heated through, about 4 minutes more. Remove the peaches from the grill.

▶ To serve, place the peaches on a platter and drizzle with the balsamic syrup. Sprinkle with the blue cheese and the chopped basil.

Serves 6.

**Cooking Tips:** When buying peaches for grilling, look for firm, slightly under-ripe peaches. Straight balsamic vinegar or store-bought balsamic syrup can be used if you are short on time.

**Do-Ahead:** The balsamic syrup can be made up to 2 weeks in advance. While it can be stored at room temperature, I prefer to keep mine chilled. It's also delicious as a salad dressing and drizzled over grilled meats.

# Grilled Pizza Margarita

*Collyn Wainwright was the first person to introduce me to grilled pizzas. It was close to ten years ago, and I still remember it: Sautéed wild mushrooms and smoked mozzarella on a slightly charred pizza crust. Heaven! The sky is the limit on variations you can make, but this is a good starter recipe.*

Vegetable oil, for the grates
Unbaked pizza dough, enough for a
    12-inch pizza
2 tablespoons olive oil, divided
Kosher salt and freshly ground black
    pepper

3/4 pound smoked mozzarella, coarsely
    shredded
1 cup cherry tomatoes, cut in half
3/4 cup pitted kalamata olives, drained
    and coarsely chopped
1/4 cup thinly sliced fresh basil

▶ Preheat a clean grill to medium with the lid closed for 8 to 10 minutes. Lightly brush the grates with oil.

▶ Let the pizza dough come to room temperature. Place the dough ball onto a baking sheet. Using your hands, gently flatten, and pull into a circle about 12 inches in diameter. Brush the crust with 1 tablespoon of olive oil, and season with the salt and pepper to taste.

▶ Transfer the dough to the grill, oiled-side down. Close the lid and cook until the dough begins to bubble on the top, about 2 minutes. Working quickly, brush the dough with the remaining oil, and season with salt and pepper to taste. Turn and top with the mozzarella, tomatoes, and olives. Close the lid again and cook until golden and crisp on the bottom and the cheese is melted, 4 to 5 minutes more.

▶ Evenly sprinkle the basil over the top of the cooked pizza. Serve immediately.

Serves 6.

**Cooking Tips:** When grilling pizzas, the lid is your best friend. Use the lid to control the heat as well as to help your toppings to cook and melt more quickly.

    Instead of making your own pizza dough, you can now find pizza dough in the refrigerated section of most markets. Another option is to pick up dough from your neighborhood pizzeria.

**Variations:** You can use this same technique with your favorite pizza toppings. Since the crust cooks rather quickly, it is best to use toppings that are precooked or thinly sliced.

    If you choose to add tomato sauce, be sure to lightly sauce your pizza. Too much liquid will result in a soggy crust.

# Grilled Salmon Dip

*This yummy dip comes from the kitchen of my friend Gay Landaiche. A touch of horseradish gives it a unique twist.*

Vegetable oil, for the grates
2 4- to 6-ounce boneless salmon fillets
2 tablespoons olive oil
Kosher salt and freshly ground black pepper
3 tablespoons cream cheese, at room temperature

2 tablespoons mayonnaise
1 teaspoon prepared horseradish
1 tablespoon freshly squeezed lemon juice
2 tablespoons finely diced red onions
3 tablespoons capers

▶ Preheat a clean grill to medium-high with the lid closed for 8 to 10 minutes. Lightly brush the grates with oil.

▶ Brush the salmon with the olive oil. Season with the salt and pepper to taste.

▶ Place the salmon on the grill, flesh side down first. Close the lid and cook for 3 to 4 minutes until golden brown and slightly charred. Turn the salmon over and grill for 3 to 5 more minutes for medium. Transfer the salmon to a platter and chill in the refrigerator until cold, about 1 hour.

▶ When the salmon is cold, remove and discard the skin. Break the salmon into very large flakes and place back on the platter.

▶ In a large bowl place the cream cheese, mayonnaise, horseradish, and lemon juice. Stir until smooth. Add the flaked salmon, red onion, and capers. Mix until well combined. Season with salt and pepper to taste. Serve chilled.

*Serves 4 to 6.*

**Cooking Tips:** This is a tasty use for leftover baked or grilled salmon. Using salmon grilled on a cedar plank (page 107) would give this dip a nice smoky flavor.
   Salmon fillets can be bought with the skin on or skin removed. Both can be used for this recipe. Even though it doesn't matter for this recipe, my rule of thumb for grilling skinless salmon fillets is to grill the flesh side first since that is the side that will be presented on the plate.

# Grilled Tomato and Vidalia Onion Bruschetta

*This fabulous recipe belongs to my sister's mother-in-law, Diane Rogol. In addition to being a bruschetta appetizer, this smoky tomato mixture is also delicious as a salsa with tortilla chips or spooned over grilled chicken or steak.*

6 large ripe tomatoes, cut into 1/4-inch slices

2 Vidalia onions, peeled and cut into 1/4-inch slices

3/4 cup olive oil, divided

1/2 cup balsamic vinegar

2 tablespoons garlic powder

1/4 cup chopped fresh basil

Kosher salt and freshly ground black pepper

Vegetable oil, for the grates

6 1/2-inch slices crusty bread, such as ciabatta

▶ In a large nonreactive bowl, place the tomatoes, onions, 1/2 cup of the oil, vinegar, garlic powder, and basil. Gently toss to combine. Season with the salt and pepper to taste. Cover and refrigerate for 1 to 4 hours.

▶ Preheat a clean grill to medium-high with the lid closed for 8 to 10 minutes. Lightly brush the grates with oil.

▶ Remove the tomatoes and onions from the marinade and shake off the excess. Discard the marinade.

▶ Place the tomatoes and onions on the grill. Close the lid and cook until soft and charred, 8 to 12 minutes per side.

▶ Place the tomatoes and onions in a large bowl. Cut into rough pieces with a knife or kitchen shears. Season with salt and pepper to taste.

▶ Brush the bread on both sides with the remaining olive oil. Grill the bread on both sides until golden brown, about 2 minutes per side.

▶ To serve, place a generous spoonful of the tomato mixture on top of each slice of bread. Serve immediately.

Serves 4 to 6.

**Cooking Tips:** The high intense heat of your typical grill is a great way to toast bread. Keep a close eye out to make sure it doesn't burn.

Concerned your onion slices might fall through the grates? Secure them with a toothpick or skewers to keep the onion together. Just remember to soak wooden toothpicks or skewers in water for at least 30 minutes before grilling.

 **Do-Ahead:** This salsa can be stored in an airtight container in the refrigerator for up to one week.

 **Marinate:** 1 to 4 hours.

# Spicy Hot Wings with Blue Cheese Dip

*Buffalo wings are the quintessential game-time favorite. They have nothing to do with a buffalo but have a lot to do with a restaurant in Buffalo, New York. Just like the original recipe, I use Frank's® RedHot® to add a fiery kick to my chicken wings.*

### For the Blue Cheese Dip:
- 1/2 cup mayonnaise
- 1/2 cup sour cream
- 1 tablespoon white wine vinegar
- 1 clove garlic, minced
- 1/2 cup crumbled blue cheese
- Kosher salt and freshly ground black pepper

### For the Spicy Hot Wings:
- Vegetable oil, for the grates
- 2 1/2 pounds chicken wings and drummettes
- 1/4 cup olive oil
- 1 tablespoon cayenne pepper
- Kosher salt and freshly ground black pepper
- 1/2 cup hot sauce
- 1/3 cup unsalted butter

▸ To make the Blue Cheese Dip: In a small bowl place the mayonnaise, sour cream, vinegar, garlic, and blue cheese and whisk until well combined. Season with the salt and pepper to taste. Cover and refrigerate until ready to serve.

▸ To make the Spicy Hot Wings: Preheat a clean grill to medium-high with the lid closed for 8 to 10 minutes. Lightly brush the grates with oil.

▸ Place the chicken wings in a large bowl. Add the olive oil and cayenne pepper and toss to coat. Generously season with the salt and pepper.

▸ Place the chicken on the grill. Close the lid and cook, turning occasionally, until cooked through and golden brown on all sides, about 20 to 25 minutes total. Remove the chicken wings from the grill and place in a large bowl.

▸ Place the hot sauce and butter in a small saucepan. Bring to a simmer over medium heat and cook until the butter has melted. Pour the warm hot sauce mixture over the chicken wings and toss to coat.

▸ Serve warm with the blue cheese dip.

Serves 6 to 8.

**Cooking Tip:** Feel free to substitute a bottled blue cheese dressing if you are short on time.

**Do-Ahead:** The blue cheese dip can be made up to 3 days in advance. Store covered in the refrigerator until ready to serve.

# Tuna Tataki

*Tataki is a Japanese cooking preparation in which beef or fish is seared on the outside and served rare with a citrusy Ponzu dipping sauce.*

### For the Ponzu Ginger Sauce:
- 1/4 cup soy sauce
- 2 tablespoons water
- 1 tablespoon rice wine vinegar
- 1 tablespoon freshly squeezed lime juice
- 1/2 tablespoon finely grated fresh ginger
- 1 scallion, thinly sliced

### For the Tuna:
- 1/4 cup sesame seeds
- 1 tablespoon coarsely ground black pepper
- 1/2 pound sushi-grade tuna loin
- 2 tablespoons sesame oil
- Kosher salt
- Vegetable oil, for the grates

▸ To make the Ponzu Ginger Sauce: In a small bowl whisk together the soy sauce, water, vinegar, lime juice, ginger, and scallions. Set aside.

▸ To make the Tuna: On a shallow plate stir together the sesame seeds and black pepper. Lightly brush the tuna with sesame oil, and season with salt to taste. Roll the tuna in the sesame seed mixture, pressing down lightly to make the coating adhere on all sides.

▸ Preheat a clean grill to medium-high with the lid closed for 8 to 10 minutes. Lightly brush the grates with oil.

▸ Place the tuna on the grill. Cook, turning once, until just seared on the outside and still rare on the inside, about 2 to 3 minutes per side.

▸ To serve, slice into 1/4-inch thick pieces. Transfer to a plate or platter and serve with the Ponzu Ginger Sauce on the side.

Serves 4.

**Cooking Tip:** I find that the easiest way (and safest way for my knuckles!) to peel the papery skin off a ginger root is to use the side of a spoon rather than a knife.

**Variation:** Not a fan of fish? This recipe can also be made with a boneless sirloin steak. Just cook the beef to medium-rare.

# Veggie Stack

*It's all about the presentation! But don't let looks fool you—this delicious appetizer is simple to make.*

1 medium eggplant, cut crosswise into
   1/4-inch thick slices
Kosher salt
4 tablespoons olive oil, divided
2 tablespoons red wine vinegar
2 tablespoons balsamic vinegar
1 medium red onion, thinly sliced

Vegetable oil, for the grates
Freshly ground black pepper
1 large tomato, cut into 1/4-inch slices
8 ounces fresh mozzarella cheese, cut into
   1/4-inch slices
12 fresh basil leaves

▸ Place the eggplant in a colander and sprinkle with the salt. Let the eggplant drain in the colander for 1 hour. Rinse and then pat dry.

▸ In a large bowl whisk together 1 tablespoon of the olive oil, the red wine vinegar, and the balsamic vinegar. Add the onions and toss to coat. Set aside and marinate at room temperature while grilling the eggplants.

▸ Preheat a clean grill to medium-high with the lid closed for 8 to 10 minutes. Lightly brush the grates with oil.

▸ Lightly brush both sides of the eggplant with the remaining olive oil and season with salt and pepper to taste. Place the eggplant slices on the grill. Close the lid and cook, turning once, until tender, about 3 to 4 minutes per side.

▸ To assemble, place 2 slices of the eggplant on the plate. Then add a tomato slice and a spoonful of the marinated red onions. Next add a slice of the fresh mozzarella and top with some basil leaves. Drizzle with extra balsamic vinegar and olive oil if desired.

Serves 4 to 6.

**Cooking Tip:** Salting eggplant removes bitterness. If cooking fresh in-season eggplant (summer months), you can omit this step.

# Poultry

For weekday meals, I need options that are quick and easy. I sometimes joke that I write my cookbooks for myself . . . but there is a hint of seriousness in that statement. Being a working parent with kids who need to be driven to after-school activities as well as helped with homework, I no longer have the luxury of spending hours preparing a meal.

Enter the grill. Grilling is a fast way to prepare many dishes. I take advantage of quick-cooking cuts of meat like chicken breasts, lamb chops, flank steak, and fish fillets for my weekday meals. All you need is a fast marinade or a tasty accompaniment to make a simple dish a knockout.

I throw meats into a marinade before I take the girls to their volleyball practice or piano lessons so the meat has time to become flavorful and tender. Homework is often done in the kitchen so that I can help my girls while I'm assembling the meal.

To take the stress out of dinnertime, I try to keep my pantry well stocked. Just because I am putting a home cooked meal on the table, it doesn't mean I can't take shortcuts! Refrigerator staples like orange juice, soy sauce, and lemons are a great way to add flavor to just about any dish. For a quick fix, save a step by using a bottled marinade or other prepared food. For a side dish, pasta, rice, and even grilled bread are quick and easy ways to round out a meal.

# Apricot-Dijon Glazed Turkey Tenderloins

*This glaze, using the pantry staples of apricot preserves and Dijon mustard, is a delicious way to add flavor to turkey, chicken, and pork.*

3/4 cup apricot preserves
2 tablespoons white wine vinegar
2 tablespoons Dijon mustard
2 turkey tenderloins (about 1 1/2 pounds)
2 tablespoons olive oil

Kosher salt and freshly ground black
   pepper
Vegetable oil, for the grates

▸ In a small saucepan whisk together the apricot preserves, vinegar, and mustard until well combined. Warm over medium heat until melted and smooth, about 3 to 5 minutes. Remove from the heat. Transfer 1/4 cup to a small bowl to glaze the turkey. Reserve the remaining sauce.

▸ Brush the tenderloins on both sides with the olive oil and generously season with the salt and pepper.

▸ Preheat a clean grill to medium-high with the lid closed for 8 to 10 minutes. Lightly brush the grates with oil.

▸ Place the turkey on the grill. Close the lid and cook, brushing with the apricot mixture the last 2 minutes of cooking per side, until no longer pink in the middle, 10 to 12 minutes per side. Remove the turkey from the grill. Let rest for 5 minutes before slicing.

▸ To serve, place the sliced meat on a plate and garnish with a generous spoonful of the reserved apricot sauce.

Serves 4.

**Cooking Tip:** A turkey tenderloin is a tender piece of white meat hidden under the turkey breast. Closer to the size of a large chicken breast, it is a faster cooking cut than the turkey breast.

**Suggested Side:** Spinach-Stuffed Portobello Mushrooms (page 193)

# BBQ Chicken

*The key to perfect barbecue chicken is to apply the sauce when the chicken is almost done. This prevents the sauce from burning. For a boost of flavor, I season my chicken with a spicy dry rub instead of just salt and pepper.*

## For the Homemade BBQ Sauce:

- 2 cups ketchup
- 1/2 cup water
- 1/3 cup apple cider vinegar
- 2 tablespoons light brown sugar
- 2 tablespoons molasses
- 1 teaspoon crushed red pepper flakes
- 1 teaspoon onion powder
- 1 teaspoon ground dry mustard
- 1 tablespoon Worcestershire sauce

## For the BBQ Chicken:

- Vegetable oil, for the grates
- 2 tablespoons paprika
- 1 tablespoon chili powder
- 1 teaspoon garlic powder
- 2 teaspoons kosher salt
- 1/2 teaspoon freshly ground black pepper
- 2 1/2 pounds mixed chicken parts, such as breasts, thighs, drumsticks, and wings
- 1 cup Homemade BBQ sauce

▶ To make the Homemade BBQ Sauce: In a large saucepan combine the ketchup, water, vinegar, brown sugar, molasses, red pepper flakes, onion powder, dry mustard, and Worcestershire sauce. Over high heat, bring the sauce to a boil. Reduce the heat to medium-low and simmer, stirring occasionally, until the sauce thickens, about 20 to 25 minutes. Measure out 1 cup of sauce. Refrigerate the remaining sauce for another time.

▶ To make the BBQ Chicken: Preheat a clean grill to medium-high with the lid closed for 8 to 10 minutes. Lightly brush the grates with oil.

▶ In a small bowl combine the paprika, chili powder, garlic powder, salt, and pepper. Generously season the chicken with the dry rub.

▶ Place the chicken on the grill. Close the lid and cook, turning once or twice, until no longer pink in the middle, 12 to 15 minutes per side. During the final 5 minutes of cooking, baste the chicken with the barbecue sauce. Remove the chicken from the grill and serve warm.

Serves 4.

**Cooking Tip:** Making a homemade barbecue sauce is very easy, but it does take time. Use your favorite bottled barbecue sauce if you prefer.

**Suggested Sides:** Pete's Baked Beans (page 195) and Grilled Lime Scallions (page 207)

# Beer Can Chicken

*This crazy cooking technique is one of my favorite ways to cook a whole chicken on the grill. The open can of beer makes some of the moistest, most succulent, flavorful chicken I've ever tasted.*

Vegetable oil, for the grates
1 whole chicken (3 1/2 to 4 pounds)
Kosher salt and freshly ground black
    pepper
2 tablespoons olive oil

2 tablespoons chopped fresh thyme (or 1
    tablespoon dried thyme leaves)
1 can (12-ounce) beer, opened and half full

▶ Preheat your grill to medium-high with the lid closed for 8 to 10 minutes. Lightly brush the grates with oil.

▶ Remove and discard the giblets and any excess fat from the chicken cavity. Rinse the chicken, inside and out, with cold water and pat dry with paper towels. Generously season the inside cavity with salt and pepper.

▶ Evenly spread the olive oil over the skin of the whole bird. Generously season the skin with salt and pepper. Sprinkle the thyme evenly over the bird.

▶ Hold the chicken upright, with the opening of the body cavity at the bottom, and position the bird on the beer can so that the chicken is sitting upright, with the can in its cavity.

▶ Turn off half the burners and place the chicken on the side of the grill with the burners off, using the legs and beer can as a tripod to support the chicken on the grill.

▶ Close the lid and cook the chicken until the skin is golden brown and the meat is cooked through, 1 1/4 to 1 1/2 hours.

▶ Using tongs, carefully transfer the chicken to a cutting board or platter, holding a metal spatula underneath the beer can for support.

▶ Let the chicken rest for 5 to 10 minutes, then carefully lift it off the can. Discard the beer. Carve the chicken and serve.

Serves 4 to 6.

**Cooking Tip:** To be sure the chicken is thoroughly cooked, insert a meat thermometer into the breast. The chicken is cooked when the breast is at least 165 degrees. If you don't have a meat thermometer, poke the chicken in the thigh with a knife; if the juices run clear, the chicken is done.

**Variation:** Want a nonalcoholic version? A can of root beer works well. So does a can of chicken stock.

**Suggested Side:** Grilled Corn and Green Bean Salad (page 151)

# Honey-Lime Chicken with Corn Slaw

*I never have any leftovers when I make this refreshing and colorful slaw! It's the perfect accompaniment for a piece of grilled chicken that has had a bath in a honey-lime marinade.*

### For the Corn Slaw:

4 ears fresh corn, shucked
1 bag (10-ounce) angel hair coleslaw
    (or finely shredded green cabbage)
1/2 cup thinly sliced red bell pepper
    (1 small pepper)
1/4 cup thinly sliced scallions
1/4 cup coarsely chopped fresh cilantro
1/3 cup freshly squeezed lime juice
2 tablespoons honey
3 tablespoons olive oil
Kosher salt and freshly ground black pepper

### For the Honey-Lime Chicken Breasts:

Vegetable oil, for the grates
2/3 cup freshly squeezed lime juice
4 tablespoons honey
2 tablespoons crushed red pepper flakes
2 cloves garlic, minced
1/4 cup olive oil
4 boneless, skinless chicken breasts
    (about 1 1/2 pounds)
Kosher salt and freshly ground black
    pepper

▶ To prepare the Corn Slaw: Over high heat, bring a large pot of salted water to a boil. Add the corn and cook until tender, about 5 to 6 minutes, and then drain. Rinse the corn with cold water until cool enough to handle. Using a sharp knife, carefully slice the kernels off the cob and discard the cobs. Place the kernels in a large salad bowl. Add the slaw, red bell peppers, scallions, and cilantro and toss.

▶ In a small bowl whisk together the lime juice, honey, and olive oil until well combined. Add the honey-lime dressing to the slaw to taste and toss to coat. Season with the salt and pepper to taste. Cover and refrigerate until ready to serve.

▶ To prepare the Honey-Lime Chicken Breasts: Preheat a clean grill to medium-high with the lid closed for 8 to 10 minutes. Lightly brush the grates with oil.

▶ In a nonreactive dish just large enough to hold the chicken in a single layer, whisk together the lime juice, honey, red pepper flakes, garlic, and olive oil. Add the chicken breasts to the marinade and toss to coat. Marinate at room temperature for 15 minutes. Remove the chicken from the marinade and shake off the excess. Discard the marinade. Generously season the chicken with the salt and pepper.

▶ Place the chicken on the grill. Close the lid and cook, turning once, until it is no longer pink in the middle, 6 to 8 minutes per side. Remove the chicken from the grill.

▶ To serve, place the chicken on the plate with a generous spoonful of corn slaw.

Serves 4.

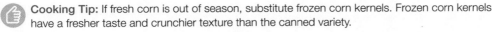 **Cooking Tip:** If fresh corn is out of season, substitute frozen corn kernels. Frozen corn kernels have a fresher taste and crunchier texture than the canned variety.

**M** **Marinate:** 15 minutes.

# Sweet Bourbon Duck Breasts

*I have to admit, I was never a fan of wild game until my husband made this dish. I think this recipe may change your mind too!*

1 tablespoon olive oil
2 cloves garlic, minced
1 tablespoon chopped fresh sage
1 tablespoon chopped fresh flat-leaf
    parsley
2 tablespoons soy sauce
1/3 cup orange juice

1 tablespoon light brown sugar
3 tablespoons bourbon
4 duck breasts (5 to 6 ounces each), skin
    scored in a crosshatch pattern
Vegetable oil, for the grates
Kosher salt and freshly ground black
    pepper

▸ In a shallow nonreactive dish just large enough to hold the duck breasts in a single layer, stir together the olive oil, garlic, sage, parsley, soy sauce, orange juice, brown sugar, and bourbon. Place the duck breasts in the marinade and gently toss until well coated. Cover, place in the refrigerator, and marinate for 2 to 4 hours.

▸ Preheat a clean grill to medium-high with the lid closed for 8 to 10 minutes. Lightly brush the grates with oil.

▸ Remove the duck from the marinade and shake off the excess. Discard the marinade. Season the duck with the salt and pepper to taste.

▸ Place the duck on the grill, skin side down. Close the lid and cook until golden brown, about 3 to 5 minutes. Turn over and cook until the desired temperature is reached, another 4 to 6 minutes for medium. Remove the duck from the grill. Let rest for 5 minutes before slicing. Serve warm.

Serves 4.

**Cooking Tips:** Duck breasts should be cooked like red meat, not chicken. They are more tender and less gamey at medium.
    This dish can be made with either wild or domestic ducks.

**M** Marinate: 2 to 4 hours.

**Suggested Sides:** Grilled Sweet Potatoes (without lime) (page 185) and Grilled Summer Squash (page 187)

# Tequila Chicken Fajitas

*My dad has perfected chicken fajitas. His secret trick for flavorful and moist chicken is to marinate it overnight.*

### For the Tequila Chicken:

1 cup freshly squeezed lemon juice
2 tablespoons tequila
1 tablespoon hot sauce
3 tablespoons olive oil
1/2 cup diced yellow onions (1 small onion)
3 cloves garlic, minced
1 tablespoon cayenne pepper
4 boneless, skinless chicken breasts
    (about 1 1/2 pounds)
Vegetable oil, for the grates
Kosher salt and freshly ground black pepper

### For the Fajitas:

1 tablespoon olive oil
1/2 cup thinly sliced red onions
    (1 small onion)
1/2 cup thinly sliced red bell pepper
    (1 small pepper)
1/2 cup thinly sliced yellow bell pepper
    (1 small pepper)
8 flour tortillas, warmed
1 cup guacamole (optional garnish)
1 cup pico de gallo (optional garnish)
1 cup shredded Monterey Jack cheese
    (optional garnish)

▸ To make the Tequila Chicken: In a shallow nonreactive dish just large enough to hold the chicken in a single layer, stir together the lemon juice, tequila, hot sauce, olive oil, onions, garlic, and cayenne pepper. Place the chicken breasts in the marinade and gently toss until well coated. Cover, place in the refrigerator, and marinate for at least 2 hours or overnight.

▸ Preheat a clean grill to medium-high with the lid closed for 8 to 10 minutes. Lightly brush the grates with oil.

▸ Remove the chicken from the marinade and shake off the excess. Discard the marinade. Season the chicken with the salt and pepper to taste.

▸ Place the chicken on the grill. Close the lid and cook, turning once, until no longer pink in the middle, 6 to 8 minutes per side. Remove

the chicken from the grill. Let rest for 5 minutes before slicing.

▸ To make the Fajitas: In a large skillet over medium-high heat, warm the olive oil until a few droplets of water sizzle when carefully sprinkled in the pan. Add the onions, red bell peppers, and yellow bell peppers. Cook, stirring frequently, until the vegetables are soft, about 5 minutes.

▸ To serve, thinly slice the chicken across the grain. Arrange the chicken and vegetables on a platter. Serve with warmed tortillas and guacamole, pico de gallo, and Monterey Jack cheese, as desired. Allow diners to make their own fajitas by putting their favorite ingredients in the tortillas.

Serves 4.

**Cooking Tip:** Did you know that your tortillas can easily be warmed on the grill? Wrap the tortillas in aluminum foil and warm on the grill over direct heat for 2 to 3 minutes.

**Marinate:** Overnight for best results. If short on time, marinate for at least 2 hours.

# Tandoori Chicken

*You don't have to have a clay oven to make tandoori chicken. I actually prefer the smoky flavor this classic Indian dish gets from a hot grill.*

1 cup nonfat plain yogurt
1 tablespoon freshly squeezed lemon juice
2 cloves garlic, minced
1 tablespoon finely grated fresh ginger
1/2 teaspoon ground coriander
1/2 teaspoon ground cumin
1/2 teaspoon ground turmeric
1/2 teaspoon paprika
1/2 teaspoon cayenne pepper

1 teaspoon garam masala
8 skinless, bone-in chicken thighs
Vegetable oil, for the grates
Kosher salt and freshly ground black
    pepper
1 package (12-ounce) naan (Indian
    flatbread)
1 cup raita

▸ In a shallow nonreactive dish just large enough to hold the chicken in a single layer, stir together the yogurt, lemon juice, garlic, ginger, coriander, cumin, turmeric, paprika, cayenne pepper, and garam masala.

▸ With a sharp knife, cut 2 to 3 deep slashes in the chicken meat. Place the chicken in the marinade and gently toss until well coated. Cover, place in the refrigerator, and marinate for at least 2 hours or overnight.

▸ Preheat a clean grill to medium-high with the lid closed for 8 to 10 minutes. Lightly brush the grates with oil.

▸ Remove the chicken from the marinade and shake off the excess. Discard the marinade. Season the chicken with the salt and pepper to taste.

▸ Place the chicken on the grill. Close the lid and cook, turning once or twice, until no longer pink in the middle, 20 to 25 minutes total.

▸ Serve with warm naan and raita on the side.

Serves 4 to 6.

**Cooking Tip:** Raita is a cucumber-yogurt sauce that is traditionally served alongside spicy Indian dishes to cool the palate. To make this condiment, combine 2 cups plain yogurt, 1 cup finely diced cucumber, 1 minced clove of garlic, 1/2 teaspoon cumin, and 2 tablespoons chopped fresh mint or cilantro.

**M** **Marinate:** Ideally overnight, but for at least 2 hours.

# Prosciutto and Fontina Stuffed Chicken Breasts

*Stuffed chicken breasts sound fancy, but they can be a cinch to make. You can use anything for stuffing—
meats, cheeses, relishes, herbs, or tapenades. Intense flavors are good since there's not room for too much.
Tom Conlee gave me the idea to use this delicious combination of prosciutto, Fontina, and herb butter. I
hope you will enjoy it as much as I do.*

4 tablespoons unsalted butter, softened
2 tablespoons minced shallots
1 tablespoon finely chopped fresh sage
2 ounces Fontina cheese, cut into 3-inch-
    by-1-inch sticks
4 slices prosciutto

4 boneless, skinless chicken breasts
    (about 1 1/2 pounds)
2 tablespoons olive oil
Kosher salt and freshly ground black
    pepper
Vegetable oil, for the grates

▸ In a small bowl stir together the butter, shallots, and sage until well combined. Set aside.

▸ Wrap each piece of cheese with a slice of prosciutto. Set aside.

▸ Place a chicken breast on a cutting board. To create a pocket, cut a slit in to the thickest part of the breast three fourths of the way through the center (about 3 1/2 inches long) and then move the knife in a fanning motion to create the pocket, being careful not to cut through to the other side. Repeat with each chicken breast.

▸ Place one tablespoon of the herb butter into each pocket and spread evenly with your fingers. Insert a wrapped cheese stick into each

pocket. Secure with a toothpick if desired.

▸ Brush the breasts on both sides with the olive oil and season with the salt and pepper to taste.

▸ Preheat a clean grill to medium-high with the lid closed for 8 to 10 minutes. Lightly brush the grates with oil.

▸ Place the chicken on the grill. Close the lid and cook, turning once, until no longer pink in the middle, 6 to 8 minutes per side. Remove the chicken from the grill. Let rest for 5 minutes before slicing. Serve warm.

Serves 4.

**Cooking Tips:** Many people butterfly a chicken breast when stuffing, but I find the pocket-method better keeps the filling inside the breast.
    When stuffing a chicken breast, you don't want to add too much filling. Approximately 1/4 cup of filling is the perfect amount.

**Variation:** Fresh thyme, rosemary, or basil would all be delicious substitutions for the sage in the herb butter.

**Suggested Sides:** Grilled Potato Salad (page 149) and Grilled Asparagus (page 183)

# Lemon-Oregano Chicken

*A mixture of fresh herbs, lemon, and garlic tucked under the skin helps to make the chicken meat extra flavorful.*

1/4 cup freshly squeezed lemon juice
3 tablespoons olive oil
3 tablespoons coarsely chopped fresh oregano
2 cloves garlic, minced
1 tablespoon freshly grated lemon zest

4 split, bone-in, skin-on chicken breasts (about 3 pounds)
Vegetable oil, for the grates
Kosher salt and freshly ground black pepper

▸ In a nonreactive dish just large enough to hold the chicken in a single layer, whisk together the lemon juice, olive oil, oregano, garlic, and lemon zest. Add the chicken breasts to the marinade and toss to coat. Marinate at room temperature for 20 to 30 minutes.

▸ Preheat a clean grill to medium-high with the lid closed for 8 to 10 minutes. Lightly brush the grates with oil.

▸ Remove the chicken from the marinade and shake off the excess. Run your fingers between the chicken and the skin to loosen the skin (be careful not to remove the skin). Evenly spread about 1/2 tablespoon of the lemon zest, oregano, and garlic from the marinade under the skin of each breast. Discard the rest of the marinade. Generously season the chicken with the salt and pepper.

▸ Place the chicken on the grill. Close the lid and cook, turning once or twice, until no longer pink in the middle, 12 to 15 minutes per side. Serve warm.

Serves 4.

**Cooking Tip:** Try other citrus herb combinations like lime-cilantro and orange-sage.

**Marinate:** 20 to 30 minutes.

**Suggested Sides:** Grilled Cherry Tomatoes with Sweet Basil Vinaigrette (page 205) and Lemony Grilled Fennel (page 189)

# Jamaican Jerk Chicken

*A couple of years ago, I had my first taste of Jamaica's famous jerk chicken. After one bite of the deliciously fiery sauce at Scotchie's, a roadside jerk shack in Montego Bay, I was hooked! My version may not be quite as fiery, but it is pretty close to the real deal.*

1 Scotch Bonnet or habanero chile
    pepper, finely chopped
1 cup thinly sliced scallions
4 cloves garlic, minced
2 tablespoons fresh thyme leaves
1 tablespoon allspice
2 tablespoons freshly ground black pepper

2 tablespoons kosher salt
2 tablespoons brown sugar
2 tablespoons distilled white vinegar
2 1/2 pounds mixed chicken parts, such
    as breasts, thighs, drumsticks, and
    wings
Vegetable oil, for the grates

▸ In a food processor or blender, combine the peppers, scallions, garlic, thyme, allspice, black pepper, salt, brown sugar, and vinegar. Place the chicken in a shallow nonreactive bowl, just large enough to hold the chicken in a single layer. Add the marinade and gently toss until well coated. Cover, place in the refrigerator, and marinate for at least 4 hours or overnight.

▸ Preheat a clean grill to medium-high with the lid closed for 8 to 10 minutes. Lightly brush the grates with oil.

▸ Remove the chicken from the marinade and shake off the excess. Discard the marinade.

▸ Place the chicken on the grill and close the lid. Cook the chicken, turning once or twice, until no longer pink in the middle, 12 to 15 minutes per side. Serve warm.

Serves 4.

**Cooking Tips:** Scotch Bonnet and habanero chile peppers are very hot and can burn your skin. Use protective gloves when handling the chiles and jerk sauce.
    Using one pepper makes the heat in this sauce perfect for my family. Add additional peppers if you want a more fiery sauce.

**M**   **Marinate:** Ideally overnight, but at least 4 hours.

**Suggested Side:** Grilled Lime Sweet Potatoes (page 185)

# Grilled Herb Chicken with Greek Tomato-Olive Relish

*A good relish can transform everyday chicken breasts into a showstopper. This Greek-inspired tomato relish is just such an example.*

### For the Greek Tomato-Olive Relish:
1 cup cherry tomatoes, quartered
1/4 cup kalamata olives, pitted and coarsely chopped
1/4 cup finely diced red onion (1/2 small onion)
1 tablespoon olive oil
1 teaspoon red wine vinegar
1/4 cup crumbled feta cheese
2 tablespoons thinly sliced fresh mint leaves

Kosher salt and freshly ground black pepper

### For the Grilled Herb Chicken:
Vegetable oil, for the grates
4 boneless, skinless chicken breasts (about 1 1/2 pounds)
4 tablespoons dried Italian seasoning
Kosher salt and freshly ground black pepper

▶ To make the Greek Tomato-Olive Relish: Place the tomatoes, olives, red onions, olive oil, and vinegar in a medium bowl. Toss to combine. Add the feta cheese and mint and gently toss to combine. Season with salt and pepper to taste. Cover and refrigerate until ready to serve.

▶ To make the Grilled Herb Chicken: Preheat a clean grill to medium-high with the lid closed for 8 to 10 minutes. Lightly brush the grates with oil.

▶ Season both sides of the chicken with the Italian seasoning, salt, and pepper. Place the chicken on the grill. Close the lid and cook, turning once, until no longer pink in the middle, 6 to 8 minutes per side.

▶ To serve, place the chicken on the plate and top with a generous spoonful of the Tomato-Olive Relish.

Serves 4.

**Cooking Tips:** To evenly cook boneless, skinless chicken breasts, I suggest pounding them to a uniform thickness before grilling.

Dried Italian seasoning is a mixture of several dry herbs. To make your own, combine 1 tablespoon each of dried basil, dried parsley, dried oregano, dried marjoram, dried thyme leaves, dried rosemary, and dried sage. Store in an airtight container in a cool, dark place for up to six months.

**Do-Ahead:** The tomato-olive relish can be made 4 hours ahead. Store covered in the refrigerator until ready to serve.

**Variation:** Fresh basil would be a delicious substitute for the fresh mint.

**Suggested Side:** Smoky Steak Fries (page 191)

# Chicken Yakitori

*These chicken skewers are a popular item on the menus of Japanese restaurants. The sweet marinade also works well on pork.*

3/4 cup soy sauce
1/2 cup mirin
1/2 cup sake
2 tablespoons finely grated fresh ginger
1 clove garlic, minced
1/4 teaspoon crushed red pepper flakes

1 1/2 pounds skinless, boneless chicken
 thighs, cut into 1 1/2-inch pieces
Vegetable oil, for the grates
Skewers (if using bamboo, soak in water
 for 30 minutes)

▶ In a medium saucepan combine the soy sauce, mirin, sake, ginger, garlic, and crushed red pepper flakes. Over high heat, bring the mixture to a boil. Reduce the heat to medium and simmer until the sauce has thickened slightly, about 8 minutes. Remove from the heat and let cool to room temperature.

▶ Put the chicken in a large bowl. Add 1/2 cup of the marinade and toss to coat. Cover, place in the refrigerator, and marinate for 30 minutes. Reserve the remaining marinade at room temperature to brush on the chicken while grilling.

▶ Preheat a clean grill to medium-high with the lid closed for 8 to 10 minutes. Lightly brush the grates with oil.

▶ Remove the chicken from the marinade and shake off the excess. Discard the marinade. Thread the chicken onto the skewers.

▶ Place the chicken on the grill. Close the lid and cook, basting with the reserved marinade and turning frequently to prevent scorching, until no longer pink in the middle, about 3 to 5 minutes on each side. Serve warm.

Serves 4.

**Cooking Tips:** Mirin is sweetened rice cooking wine. It is found in the international section of most large supermarkets.
 Most of the alcohol in the sake evaporates when the marinade is brought to a boil. Unseasoned rice wine vinegar can be substituted for the sake, if you prefer.

**Marinate:** 30 minutes.

**Suggested Side:** Grilled Bok Choy with Ponzu Ginger Sauce (page 213)

# Chicken Drumsticks with Mustard BBQ Sauce

*The combination of sweet and tangy flavors in this mustard-based barbecue sauce brings out the absolute best in grilled chicken or pork.*

### For the Mustard BBQ Sauce:
   1/2 cup prepared yellow mustard
   1/3 cup apple cider vinegar
   1/4 cup light brown sugar
   1 tablespoon ground dry mustard
   1/2 teaspoon cayenne pepper

### For the Chicken Drumsticks:
   Vegetable oil, for the grates
   12 chicken drumsticks
   2 tablespoons olive oil
   Kosher salt and freshly ground black
      pepper

▶ To make the Mustard BBQ sauce: In a large saucepan combine the mustard, vinegar, brown sugar, dry mustard, and cayenne pepper. Over high heat, bring the sauce to a boil. Reduce the heat to medium-low and simmer, stirring occasionally, until the sauce thickens, about 15 minutes.

▶ To make the Chicken Drumsticks: Preheat a clean grill to medium-high with the lid closed for 8 to 10 minutes. Lightly brush the grates with oil.

▶ Lightly brush the chicken with the olive oil. Generously season the chicken with the salt and pepper.

▶ Place the chicken on the grill. Close the lid and cook, turning once or twice, until no longer pink in the middle, about 15 to 18 minutes per side. During the final 5 minutes of cooking, baste the chicken with the Mustard BBQ sauce. Remove the chicken from grill and serve warm.

Serves 4.

**Do-Ahead:** The Mustard BBQ sauce can be made up to 3 days in advance. Cover and refrigerate until ready to serve. Reheat over medium-low heat.

**Suggested Side:** Cajun Grilled Okra (page 181)

# Meat

With all good food, you can truly taste a difference when a dish is made with love and care. Food can nourish the body *and* the soul. Think about it. Don't some dishes evoke memories of good times with friends and family?

Because most of the recipes in this book are simple preparations, you want to start with high-quality ingredients. The key to delicious food is simple: use fresh and in-season ingredients. Let flavor be your guide when choosing what goes into your dishes.

The love in preparing a meal can extend beyond the doors of your kitchen. Thanks to my local farmers markets, I have gotten to know the people who raise and grow the food I feed to my family.

The beef I buy comes from a family-run farm that raises their cattle with care and compassion. Michael and Charline Lenagar of Neola Farms take great pride in their Black Angus cattle. Since they raise their cattle from birth until time for the slaughterhouse, Charline can even tell you the lineage back to several generations of the cow you are enjoying!

Many of the farmers I have befriended have been gracious enough to invite me to their farms. I always bring my children since it is a unique opportunity for them to see where their food comes from. These visits have been a hands-on educational experience that I hope will stay with them for a lifetime. It's sad that most kids today think that food comes in a box!

No matter where you live, finding the freshest ingredients, preferably locally grown, will make even your simplest dishes unforgettable.

# Honey-Teriyaki Pork Tenderloin

*My friend Ernie Mellor is a pitmaster extraordinaire. After winning famous barbecue contest awards, such as the Memphis in May World Championship Barbecue Cooking Contest, he went on to open his own barbecue catering business, Hog Wild. This recipe is one he often serves from his gourmet catering division, A Moveable Feast.*

2 cups teriyaki sauce
1/2 cup honey
1/4 cup chopped scallions
1 tablespoon finely grated fresh ginger, or
    1 teaspoon ground ginger
3 cloves garlic, minced

1 tablespoon coarsely ground black
    pepper
2 1-pound pork tenderloins, trimmed
Vegetable oil, for the grates
Kosher salt and freshly ground black
    pepper

▸ In a shallow nonreactive dish just large enough to hold the pork in a single layer, combine the teriyaki sauce, honey, scallions, ginger, garlic, and pepper. Place the pork in the marinade and turn until well coated. Cover, place in the refrigerator, and marinate for at least 30 minutes or as long as overnight.

▸ Preheat a clean grill to medium-high with the lid closed for 8 to 10 minutes. Lightly brush the grates with oil.

▸ Remove the pork from the marinade and shake off the excess. Discard the marinade. Season the pork with salt and freshly ground black pepper to taste.

▸ Place the pork on the grill. Close the lid and cook, turning several times, until they are well browned on all sides and cooked to the desired temperature, about 20 minutes total for medium. Let rest 5 minutes before slicing and serving warm.

Serves 4.

**Do-Ahead:** The marinade can be made up to one day in advance. Cover and refrigerate until ready to use.

**Variation:** This marinade is also delicious on chicken.

**Marinate:** For at least 30 minutes or as long as overnight.

# Balsamic Beef Tenderloin

*The first time I had this flavorful beef tenderloin, I knew I had to get the recipe. Thanks to Beba and Ricardo Heros for sharing it with me so I can share it with you.*

8 cloves garlic, minced
1 teaspoon salt
1 tablespoon freshly squeezed lemon juice
1 tablespoon balsamic vinegar
1/3 cup red wine vinegar
1/3 cup olive oil

1/3 cup dried Italian seasoning
1/4 cup freshly ground black pepper
1 beef tenderloin (about 3 pounds), trimmed
Vegetable oil, for the grates

▶ Mix the garlic, salt, lemon juice, balsamic vinegar, red wine vinegar, olive oil, Italian seasoning, and pepper in a small bowl until well combined.

▶ Place the meat in a nonreactive dish and pour the marinade evenly over the meat, cover and refrigerate. Marinate for at least 2 hours or up to 6 hours. Remove from the refrigerator 30 minutes before grilling.

▶ Preheat a clean grill to medium-high with the lid closed for 8 to 10 minutes. Lightly brush the grates with oil.

▶ Remove the tenderloin from the marinade. Discard the marinade.

▶ Place the tenderloin on the grill. Close the lid and cook, turning several times, until the meat is well browned on all sides and cooked to the desired temperature, 20 to 25 minutes for medium-rare and 25 to 30 minutes for medium.

▶ Transfer to a cutting board and let rest for 5 minutes before slicing. Serve warm.

Serves 6.

**Cooking Tip:** An instant-read meat thermometer is the best way to tell if your tenderloin is ready. For medium-rare, the thermometer should read 130°F since the temperature will rise another 5 to 10 degrees while the tenderloin is resting.

**Do-Ahead:** The marinade can be made up to one day in advance. Cover and refrigerate until ready to use.

**Variation:** Don't have time to marinate your tenderloin? Just brush with olive oil and generously season with salt and pepper. Follow the cooking directions as listed above.

**Marinate:** For at least 2 hours or up to 6 hours.

**Suggested Sides:** Asparagus and Cherry Tomato Salad (page 133) or Mediterranean Quinoa Salad (page 145)

# Blue Cheese Stuffed Filet Mignon

*This steakhouse favorite couldn't be any easier to make at home.*

Vegetable oil, for the grates
4 6-ounce filet mignons, each about
    1 1/4-inches thick
2 tablespoons olive oil

Kosher salt and freshly ground black
    pepper
3/4 cup crumbled blue cheese

▸ Preheat a clean grill to medium-high with the lid closed for 8 to 10 minutes. Lightly brush the grates with oil.

▸ Lightly brush the filets with the olive oil. Generously season with the salt and pepper.

▸ Place the steaks on the grill. Close the lid and cook until they are the desired temperature, 5 to 6 minutes per side for medium-rare or 6 to 7 minutes per side for medium. Cut a slit in the top of the filet and stuff with about 3 tablespoons of blue cheese. Close the lid and cook for 1 minute more. Remove the steak from the heat and set aside to rest for 5 minutes before serving.

Serves 4.

**Cooking Tip:** When cutting the slit in the top of the filet, be sure not to cut all the way through. I recommend 1/2- to 3/4-inch deep for a 1 1/4–inch thick filet.

# Cowboy T-Bone with Whiskey Butter

*Weren't the favorite libations of the Old West a cup of Joe and a swig of whiskey? This hearty steak recipe gets a delicious twist from both of these cowboy favorites.*

## For the Whiskey Butter:

- 1 cup unsalted butter (2 sticks), room temperature
- 1 teaspoon Dijon mustard
- 4 teaspoons whiskey (or bourbon)
- 1 tablespoon finely diced shallots
- 2 tablespoons finely chopped fresh flat-leaf parsley
- Pinch of kosher salt

## For the Cowboy T-Bone:

- 1 tablespoon kosher salt
- 1 teaspoon paprika
- 1 teaspoon garlic powder
- 1 teaspoon freshly ground black pepper
- 1 teaspoon dried thyme leaves
- 1 teaspoon finely ground coffee beans
- 4 10-ounce T-bone steaks, each about 1-inch thick
- 2 tablespoons olive oil
- Vegetable oil, for the grates

▶ To make the Whiskey Butter: In the bowl of an electric mixer using the paddle attachment, beat the butter until light and fluffy. Add the mustard, whiskey, shallots, parsley, and salt and mix until thoroughly combined.

▶ Spoon the mixture in the shape of a log onto a piece of parchment paper. Fold the paper over itself. Using your hands, shape the butter into a cylinder about 1 1/2 inches wide (almost like making a Tootsie Roll). Once it is shaped, twist the edges of the paper to seal it. Place it in the freezer to set, about 20 minutes. Transfer it to the refrigerator until ready to serve.

▶ When ready to serve, slice the roll into 1/4-inch rounds and remove the parchment. (Only 4 slices of compound butter are needed for this recipe.)

▶ To make the Cowboy T-Bones: In a small bowl whisk together the salt, paprika, garlic powder, pepper, thyme, and coffee grounds. Season both sides of the steak with the rub. Drizzle the olive oil over the top. Marinate at room temperature for 30 minutes.

▶ Preheat a clean grill to medium-high with the lid closed for 8 to 10 minutes. Lightly brush the grates with oil.

▶ Place the steaks on the grill. Close the lid and cook, turning once, until the desired temperature is reached, 4 to 6 minutes per side for medium-rare or 5 to 7 minutes per side for medium. Remove the steaks from the heat and set aside to rest for 5 minutes.

▶ Serve with a slice of Whiskey Butter on top.

Serves 4.

**Do-Ahead:** The Whiskey Butter can be stored for up to 1 month in the freezer.

**Marinate:** 30 minutes.

**Suggested Sides:** Smoky Steak Fries (page 191) and Grilled Cherry Tomatoes with Sweet Basil Vinaigrette (page 205)

# Honey-Rosemary Pork Chops

*I think this may be my husband's favorite dish. He'd make these pork chops every night if I'd let him!*

Vegetable oil, for the grates
1/4 cup honey
4 tablespoons olive oil, divided
2 tablespoons chopped fresh rosemary

4 6-ounce boneless pork chops, each
   about 3/4-inch thick
Kosher salt and freshly ground black
   pepper

▶ Preheat a clean grill to medium-high with the lid closed for 8 to 10 minutes. Lightly brush the grates with oil.

▶ In a small bowl whisk together the honey, 2 tablespoons of the olive oil, and rosemary. Transfer half to a small bowl to glaze the pork chops. Reserve the remaining glaze to brush on the cooked chops.

▶ Lightly brush the pork chops with the remaining olive oil. Season with the salt and pepper to taste. Lightly brush the honey-rosemary glaze on both sides of each chop.

▶ Place the chops on the grill. Close the lid and cook until golden brown and slightly charred, about 5 to 6 minutes. Turn the chops over and lightly brush with the reserved glaze. Continue cooking for 6 to 8 more minutes for medium. Remove the chops from the heat, brush with more glaze, and set aside to rest for 5 minutes before serving.

Serves 4.

**Cooking Tip:** If you like the sweetness of the honey-rosemary glaze, feel free to drizzle a little more over the pork chops just before serving.

**Suggested Sides:** Cajun Grilled Okra (page 181) or Grilled Zucchini Ribbons (page 203)

# Pork Souvlaki

*The lemony marinade for this traditional Greek dish gives the meat a bright and fresh flavor. I like to serve it with grilled pita bread.*

1/4 cup freshly squeezed lemon juice
2 tablespoons red wine vinegar
3 tablespoons olive oil
2 teaspoons dried oregano
2 cloves garlic, minced
1 1/2 pounds pork tenderloin, trimmed and
    cut into 1-inch cubes

Vegetable oil, for the grates
Kosher salt and freshly ground black
    pepper
Skewers (if using bamboo, soak in water
    for 30 minutes)
Grilled pita bread

▸ In a shallow nonreactive dish just large enough to hold the pork in a single layer, combine the lemon juice, vinegar, olive oil, oregano, and garlic. Place the pork in the marinade and gently toss until well coated. Cover, place in the refrigerator, and marinate for at least 30 minutes or as long as overnight.

▸ Preheat a clean grill to medium-high with the lid closed for 8 to 10 minutes. Lightly brush the grates with oil.

▸ Remove the pork from the marinade and shake off the excess. Discard the marinade. Season the pork with the salt and pepper to taste. Thread the pork cubes onto the skewers.

▸ Place the skewers on the grill. Close the lid and cook, turning once or twice, until the cubes are well browned on all sides and cooked through, 8 to 12 minutes total. Serve warm.

Serves 4.

**(V) Variation:** In Greece, this dish is often also made with lamb.

**(M) Marinate:** At least 30 minutes or as long as overnight.

# Weekday Ribs

*People in Memphis take their barbecue seriously. In fact, many have perfected it to an art form. I am not here to argue that "low and slow" (the mantra for cooking ribs in the South) is not the best, but the reality is that I just don't have time to tend to the grill for hours on a busy weeknight. By baking the ribs first in the oven, I have taken the guesswork out of making flavorful and tender ribs.*

1/4 cup prepared yellow mustard
1/4 cup barbecue dry rub seasoning
2 slabs pork baby back ribs (about 3 to 4
    pounds total)

Vegetable oil, for the grates
1 1/2 cups barbecue sauce

▸ Preheat an oven to 300°F.

▸ Place each slab of ribs on a double layer of aluminum foil. Evenly slather both sides with the mustard. Generously season the ribs with the dry rub. Tightly wrap each slab of ribs in the foil and place on a baking sheet. Place in the oven and cook until the meat pulls away from the bone and is easily pierced with the tip of a sharp knife, 1 to 1 1/2 hours.

▸ Preheat a clean grill to medium-high with the lid closed for 8 to 10 minutes. Lightly brush the grates with oil.

▸ Carefully remove the ribs from the foil, pouring off any liquid. Brush the barbecue sauce generously on both sides of the ribs.

▸ Place the ribs on the grill. Close the lid and cook the ribs until the sauce begins to bubble and brown around the edges, about 4 to 5 minutes per side. Serve the ribs with extra sauce, if desired.

Serves 4.

**Cooking Tips:** For Memphis-style dry ribs, leave off the barbecue sauce and add extra dry rub prior to grilling the ribs.
    Use your favorite homemade or bottled barbecue sauce in this recipe. For my Homemade BBQ Sauce, see page 45.

# Skirt Steak Fajitas

*My sister Susan Rogol makes the best skirt steak fajitas. Don't be tempted to add to the simple marinade . . . as she says, "Why mess with success?!"*

### For the Skirt Steak:
1/4 cup freshly squeezed lime juice
1/4 cup soy sauce
2 tablespoons olive oil
2 tablespoons crushed red pepper flakes
2 pounds skirt steak, trimmed
Vegetable oil, for the grates
Kosher salt and freshly ground black pepper

### For the Fajitas:
1 tablespoon vegetable oil

1/2 cup thinly sliced red onions (1 small onion)
1/2 cup thinly sliced red bell peppers (1 small pepper)
1/2 cup thinly sliced yellow bell peppers (1 small pepper)
8 flour tortillas, warmed
1 cup guacamole (optional garnish)
1 cup pico de gallo (optional garnish)
1 cup shredded Monterey Jack cheese (optional garnish)

▶ To make the Skirt Steak: In a shallow nonreactive dish just large enough to hold the meat in a single layer, stir together the lime juice, soy sauce, olive oil, and red pepper flakes. Place the steak in the marinade and gently toss until well coated. Marinate at room temperature for 30 minutes, but not more than 1 hour.

▶ Preheat a clean grill to medium-high with the lid closed for 8 to 10 minutes. Lightly brush the grates with oil.

▶ Remove the steak from the marinade and shake off the excess. Discard the marinade. Season with the salt and pepper to taste.

▶ Place the steak on the grill. Close the lid and cook, turning once, until the desired temperature is reached, 4 to 5 minutes per side for medium-rare or 5 to 6 minutes per side for medium. Remove the steak from the heat and set aside to rest for 5 minutes.

▶ To make the Fajitas: In a large skillet over medium-high heat, warm the oil until a few droplets of water sizzle when carefully sprinkled in the pan. Add the onions, red bell peppers, and yellow bell peppers. Cook, stirring frequently, until the vegetables are soft, about 5 minutes.

▶ To serve, thinly slice the steak across the grain. Arrange the steak and vegetables on a platter. Serve with the warmed tortillas and the guacamole, pico de gallo, and Monterey Jack cheese. Allow diners to make their own fajitas by putting their favorite ingredients in the tortillas.

Serves 6.

**Cooking Tip:** Skirt steak is a long, flat cut that is prized for flavor but is tougher than many other steak cuts. Just like flank steak (which is a perfect substitute), it becomes tender when marinated and sliced across the grain.

**Marinate:** 30 minutes, but not more than 1 hour.

# Lamb Lollipops with Pomegranate Glaze

*Frenched lamb rib chops are often called lollipop chops because they are eaten using the bone as a "handle." With this gorgeously rich glaze, they make a fabulous party dish.*

### For the Pomegranate Glaze:
4 cups pomegranate juice
1/2 cup sugar

### For the Lamb Lollipops:
Vegetable oil, for the grates
12 3-ounce baby rib lamb chops, frenched

2 tablespoons olive oil
Kosher salt and freshly ground black
  pepper
1/2 cup pomegranate seeds (optional)

▶ To make the Pomegranate Glaze: Place the pomegranate juice and sugar in a medium saucepan. Cook over medium-high heat, stirring occasionally, until the sugar has completely dissolved. Once the sugar has dissolved, reduce the heat to medium-low and cook until the mixture has reduced and is the consistency of syrup, 15 to 20 minutes. Remove from the heat. Pour half the mixture into a separate bowl and set aside for serving.

▶ To make the Lamb Lollipops: Preheat a clean grill to medium-high with the lid closed for 8 to 10 minutes. Lightly brush the grates with oil.

▶ Lightly brush the chops with the olive oil. Generously season with the salt and pepper.

▶ Place the chops on the grill. Close the lid and cook until golden brown, about 3 to 4 minutes. Turn the chops over and lightly brush with the glaze. Continue cooking for 3 to 4 more minutes for medium-rare or 4 to 5 more minutes for medium. Remove the chops from the heat, brush with more glaze, and set aside to rest for 5 minutes.

▶ To serve, place 3 chops on a plate and drizzle with the reserved pomegranate glaze. Garnish with pomegranate seeds if desired.

Serves 4.

**Cooking Tip:** To "french" a bone means to cut the meat away from the end of a rib or chop, so that part of the bone is exposed. This is done with racks of lamb, beef, and pork, primarily for looks. I like it for this recipe because it makes the lamb chops easier to pick up and eat as a finger food.

**Do-Ahead:** The Pomegranate glaze can be made up to 3 days in advance. Store in the refrigerator until ready to use. Reheat in a small saucepan before using in this recipe.

**Suggested Side:** Miso Eggplant (page 197)

# Lamb Loin Chops with Mint Salsa Verde

*Lamb chops and mint are a traditional pairing. Instead of using mint jelly, I prefer this fresher mint salsa verde.*

### For the Mint Salsa Verde:

2 cups finely chopped fresh mint leaves
1/4 cup finely chopped fresh flat-leaf
    parsley
1 clove garlic, minced
1 tablespoon capers
1/4 teaspoon crushed red pepper flakes
4 tablespoons olive oil
Kosher salt and freshly ground black
    pepper

### For the Lamb Loin Chops:

Vegetable oil, for the grates
8 6-ounce lamb loin chops, each about
    1-inch thick
4 tablespoons olive oil
Kosher salt and freshly ground black
    pepper

▶ To make the Mint Salsa Verde: In a small bowl stir together the mint, parsley, garlic, capers, red pepper flakes, and olive oil. Season with the salt and pepper to taste. Set aside at room temperature.

▶ To make the Lamb Loin Chops: Preheat a clean grill to medium-high with the lid closed for 8 to 10 minutes. Lightly brush the grates with oil.

▶ Pat the lamb dry with paper towels. Lightly brush the chops with the olive oil. Generously season with the salt and pepper.

▶ Place the chops on the grill. Close the lid and cook, turning once, until the desired temperature is reached, 6 to 8 minutes per side for medium-rare or 7 to 9 minutes per side for medium. Remove the chops from the heat and set aside to rest for 5 minutes.

▶ To serve, place 2 chops on a plate and garnish with a generous spoonful of the Mint Salsa Verde.

Serves 4.

**Variation:** This Mint Salsa Verde would also be delicious with other cuts of lamb, such as leg of lamb and frenched lamb rib chops.

**Suggested Side:** Grilled Polenta Cakes (page 211)

# Korean Barbecue Lettuce Wraps

*These lettuce wraps from the kitchen of my friend Macrae Schaffler are sure to become a favorite in your house. She and her husband regularly enjoyed Korean barbecue when they lived in Los Angeles, but when they moved to Tennessee they had to make it at home. Perfect for a weeknight supper or a dinner party, this recipe couldn't be any simpler.*

2 tablespoons Asian garlic chili sauce
2 tablespoons toasted sesame oil
2/3 cup rice wine vinegar
1 cup soy sauce
2 teaspoons sugar
2 teaspoons sesame seeds
3 tablespoons grated fresh ginger
1/4 cup chopped fresh cilantro
6 boneless breakfast pork chops, small,
thin cuts, about 1/4-inch thick each
(about 1 1/2 pounds total)
Vegetable oil, for the grates
1 large head butter lettuce, leaves
separated
Fresh mint leaves (optional)
Lime wedges (optional)
Grated carrots (optional)
Chopped scallions (optional)

▶ In a shallow nonreactive dish just large enough to hold the meat in a single layer, stir together the chili sauce, sesame oil, vinegar, soy sauce, sugar, sesame seeds, ginger, and cilantro. Reserve 1 cup of the mixture as a sauce and refrigerate until ready to use.

▶ Place the pork chops in the marinade and toss to coat. Marinate at room temperature for 20 minutes.

▶ Preheat a clean grill to medium-high with the lid closed for 8 to 10 minutes. Lightly brush the grates with oil.

▶ Remove the pork chops from the marinade and shake off the excess. Discard the marinade.

▶ Place the pork chops on the grill. Close the lid and cook, turning once, until no longer pink in the middle, about 3 to 5 minutes on each side. Remove from the grill and slice into thin strips.

▶ To serve, take 1 lettuce leaf at a time and place a spoonful of the sliced pork into the center. Garnish with the reserved sauce and your desired toppings.

▶ Wrap the lettuce around the filling. Serve immediately.

Serves 4.

**Cooking Tip:** These wraps work best with the large, pliable lettuce leaves. I like to use butter lettuce, but Boston Bibb, red leaf, and even iceberg lettuces would also work. No matter which lettuce you choose, be sure to dry the lettuce well before using it for the wraps.

**Do-Ahead:** Make and refrigerate the marinade up to 3 days in advance. Prepare the garnishes and wrap separately in resealable plastic bags a day in advance.

**V** **Variation:** If there's no lettuce in the house, put the fillings over rice for a tasty rice bowl dish.

**M** **Marinate:** 20 minutes.

# Grilled Pork Loin Chops with a Dijon-Citrus Sauce

*This dish really makes a statement at a dinner party, yet it is so easy to make. Thanks to the ever-talented grill master Will Sharp for sharing this flavorful dish.*

2 tablespoons dry white wine
1/3 cup Dijon mustard
1 tablespoon Worcestershire sauce
1 cup coarsely chopped mandarin orange
　　segments, with juice
1 tablespoon fresh thyme, or 1 teaspoon
　　dried thyme leaves
1 tablespoon chopped fresh rosemary
1 clove garlic, minced

Dash of cayenne pepper
4 8-ounce bone-in, center-cut pork loin
　　chops, each about 1-inch thick
Vegetable oil, for the grates
Kosher salt and freshly ground black
　　pepper
1 cup French fried onions

▸ In a shallow nonreactive dish just large enough to hold the meat in a single layer, stir together the white wine, mustard, Worcestershire, oranges with juice, thyme, rosemary, garlic, and cayenne pepper. Reserve 1 cup of the mixture as a sauce and refrigerate until ready to use.

▸ Place the pork chops in the marinade and gently toss until well coated. Cover, refrigerate, and marinate for at least 2 hours or overnight. Remove from the refrigerator 30 minutes before cooking.

▸ Preheat a clean grill to medium-high with the lid closed for 8 to 10 minutes. Lightly brush the grates with oil.

▸ Remove the chops from the marinade and shake off the excess. Discard the marinade. Season the chops with the salt and pepper to taste.

▸ Place the chops on the grill. Close the lid and cook, turning once, until the desired temperature is reached, 6 to 8 minutes per side for medium. Remove the chops from the grill. Let rest for 5 minutes before serving.

▸ Place the reserved sauce in a small saucepan and reheat over medium-low heat.

▸ To serve, place a spoonful of sauce over each chop and garnish with French fried onions.

Serves 4.

**Cooking Tip:** Most people associate French fried onions with holiday casseroles. But I keep a can of them in my pantry year-round to add flavor to dishes such as this one.

**Marinate:** 2 hours or overnight.

**Suggested Side:** Grilled Asparagus (page 183)

# Grilled Filets with Gremolata

*Gremolata is a chopped herb condiment typically made of garlic, parsley, and lemon zest. Traditionally served with the Italian braised veal shank dish Osso Bucco, the refreshing flavor of gremolata makes it a delicious accompaniment to any meat or seafood dish.*

## For the Gremolata:

- 6 tablespoons finely chopped fresh flat-leaf parsley
- 4 tablespoons finely chopped fresh cilantro
- 1 clove garlic, minced
- 1 teaspoon freshly grated lemon zest
- 2 teaspoons freshly squeezed lemon juice
- 4 tablespoons olive oil
- Kosher salt and freshly ground black pepper

## For the Grilled Filets:

- Vegetable oil, for the grates
- 4 5- to 6-ounce filet mignons, each about 1 1/4-inches thick
- 2 tablespoons olive oil
- Kosher salt and freshly ground black pepper

▸ To make the Gremolata: In a small bowl stir together the parsley, cilantro, garlic, lemon zest, lemon juice, and olive oil. Season with the salt and pepper to taste. Set aside at room temperature.

▸ To make the Grilled Filets: Preheat a clean grill to medium-high with the lid closed for 8 to 10 minutes. Lightly brush the grates with oil.

▸ Lightly brush the steaks with the olive oil. Generously season the steaks with the salt and pepper. Place the steaks on the grill. Close the lid and cook, turning once, until the desired temperature is reached, 5 to 6 minutes per side for medium-rare or 6 to 7 minutes per side for medium. Remove the steaks from the heat and set aside to rest for 5 minutes. To serve, place on a plate and garnish with a generous spoonful of the Gremolata.

Serves 4.

**Do-Ahead:** The gremolata can be made up to one day ahead. Cover and refrigerate until ready to use. Since the olive oil will congeal when refrigerated, let this sauce come to room temperature before serving.

**Suggested Side:** Grilled Lime Sweet Potatoes (page 185)

# Ginger-Soy Flank Steak

*This has been my go-to flank steak recipe for years. It's full of flavor and uses ingredients I always have in the fridge. I hope you enjoy it as much as I do.*

1/2 cup soy sauce
1/4 cup white wine vinegar
3 tablespoons freshly squeezed lime juice
3 scallions, thinly sliced
1 tablespoon finely grated fresh ginger
1/4 teaspoon crushed red pepper flakes

1 flank steak (about 1 1/2 pounds)
Vegetable oil, for the grates
Kosher salt and freshly ground black
　　pepper

▶ In a shallow nonreactive dish just large enough to hold the meat, stir together the soy sauce, vinegar, lime juice, scallions, ginger, and red pepper flakes. Place the flank steak in the marinade and turn to coat. Marinate at room temperature for 20 to 30 minutes.

▶ Preheat a clean grill to medium-high with the lid closed for 8 to 10 minutes. Lightly brush the grates with oil.

▶ Remove the flank steak from the marinade, shaking off the excess liquid. Discard the marinade. Generously season the steak with the salt and pepper.

▶ Place the steak on the grill. Close the lid and cook, turning once, until the desired temperature is reached, 4 to 5 minutes per side for medium-rare or 5 to 6 minutes per side for medium. Remove the steak from the heat and set aside to rest for 5 minutes. Thinly slice across the grain before serving.

Serves 4.

**Cooking Tip:** To save dirtying a dish, I often marinate my meats in a resealable plastic bag. Just place all the ingredients in the bag, add the meat, and turn the bag over half way though the marinating time.

**Do-Ahead:** The steak can be marinated for up to 4 hours. If marinating for longer than 30 minutes, cover it and refrigerate. Let it come to room temperature before grilling.

**M** **Marinate:** 20 to 30 minutes, but not more than 4 hours.

# Chili-Rubbed Strip Steak with Lime-Chipotle Sauce

*A zesty rub and chipotle sauce adds pizzazz to a simple grilled steak.*

### For the Lime-Chipotle Sauce:
- 3/4 cup mayonnaise
- 1/3 cup sour cream
- 2 tablespoons freshly squeezed lime juice
- 1 can chipotle chiles in adobo
- 1 tablespoon adobo sauce (from the can of chipotle chiles)
- Kosher salt and freshly ground black pepper

### For the Chili-Rubbed Strip Steak:
- 1 tablespoon chili powder
- 1/2 tablespoon paprika
- 1 tablespoon freshly ground black pepper
- 1 tablespoon light brown sugar
- 1 teaspoon kosher salt
- 4 8-ounce strip steaks, each about 1-inch thick
- 2 tablespoons olive oil
- Vegetable oil, for the grates

▸ To make the Lime-Chipotle Sauce: In a food processor, puree the mayonnaise, sour cream, lime juice, chipotle chiles, and adobo sauce until smooth. Season with the salt and pepper to taste. Cover and refrigerate until ready to serve.

▸ To make the Chili-Rubbed Strip Steaks: In a small bowl whisk together the chili powder, paprika, black pepper, brown sugar, and salt. Season both sides of the steak with the rub. Drizzle the olive oil over the top. Marinate at room temperature for 30 minutes.

▸ Preheat a clean grill to medium-high with the lid closed for 8 to 10 minutes. Lightly brush the grates with oil.

▸ Place the steaks on the grill. Close the lid and cook, turning once, until the desired temperature is reached, 4 to 6 minutes per side for medium-rare or 6 to 7 minutes for medium. Remove the steaks from the heat and set aside to rest for 5 minutes.

▸ Serve with the Lime Chipotle Sauce on the side.

Serves 4.

**Cooking Tip:** Chipotle chiles usually are sold canned and packed in adobo sauce. They are available in many supermarkets as well as Latin markets and specialty food stores. Freeze what you don't need in this recipe for another time.

**Ⓜ Marinate:** 30 minutes.

**Suggested Sides:** Grilled Lime Sweet Potatoes (page 185) and Grilled Lime Scallions (page 207)

# Seafood

I will never forget the first time I had to clean a fish! I was in culinary school at Le Cordon Bleu in Paris, France. We walked into class, and our instructor dramatically plopped a whole sea bass on my cutting board. Spoiled by the conveniences of supermarket fish counters, I thought, "Eww! What in the world do I do with this?!"

But thanks to my determination, I quickly learned how to gut, scale, and filet that fish—as well as the succession of different seafood that came across my cutting board that week. I think those French chefs loved seeing the looks of disgust on their young American students' faces as whole animals were dropped on our cutting boards for us to butcher!

At home, I'll probably never have to de-scale a large fish or pluck a chicken, but I am thankful for that education. I truly have an appreciation for butchers and fishmongers—and am so thankful they are there to do that "dirty work!"

A lot of people are intimidated by the idea of cooking fish. They are scared it will be too "fishy." But in my opinion, fish is one of the easiest dishes to prepare. It cooks so quickly that it is the ideal choice when you are wanting to get dinner on the table fast.

When armed with a few basic facts, you will be cooking fish like a pro.

- **Smell it!** When buying fish, ask to smell it. The fish should smell more like the ocean than dead fish. If it smells overly fishy, that means it is past its prime and will taste overly fishy too.
- **Don't overcook it!** Fish should be treated like red meat. Overcooking will give your fish a strong fishy taste and odor. It is best served at medium-temperature.
- **Marinate it!** Marinating fish will add moisture and flavor. However, keep in mind that fish are delicate. They should never be marinated longer than one hour.

# Blackened Swordfish with Fresh Corn and Tomato Relish

*Because of its meaty texture, swordfish filets are perfect for grilling. Grouper would also work well in this recipe.*

### For the Fresh Corn and Tomato Relish:
    1 tablespoon olive oil
    4 ears fresh corn, shucked and kernels
        removed
    2 large tomatoes, diced
    Kosher salt and freshly ground black
        pepper
    1/4 cup chopped fresh basil

### For the Blackened Swordfish:
    Vegetable oil, for the grates
    4 1-inch-thick swordfish steaks
    4 tablespoons blackened seasoning

▶ To make the Fresh Corn and Tomato Relish: In a large skillet over medium-high heat, warm the olive oil until a few droplets of water sizzle when carefully sprinkled in the pan. Add the corn and tomatoes. Sauté, stirring occasionally, until lightly browned, about 3 to 4 minutes. Season with the salt and pepper to taste. Remove from the heat and stir in the basil. Cover to keep warm until ready to serve.

▶ To make the Blackened Swordfish: Preheat a clean grill to medium-high with the lid closed for 8 to 10 minutes. Lightly brush the grates with oil.

▶ Season both sides of the swordfish steaks with the blackened seasoning.

▶ Place the swordfish on the grill. Close the lid and cook, turning once, until medium, 4 to 5 minutes per side.

▶ To serve, place the swordfish on the plate and top with a generous spoonful of the relish.

Serves 4.

**Cooking Tips:** If you would like to make your own blackened seasoning, it's really not hard to do. Just whisk together 2 teaspoons paprika and 1/2 teaspoon each of dried thyme leaves, cayenne pepper, sugar, salt, and black pepper. For a little less heat, reduce the amount of cayenne and black pepper. This mixture will store for several weeks, tightly sealed, in your spice cabinet.
   If fresh corn is not available, substitute frozen corn kernels. Frozen corn kernels have a fresher taste and crunchier texture than the canned variety.

**Variation:** Fresh cilantro would be a delicious substitute for the fresh basil.

# Canoe Trout

*In his next life, my husband is going to be a fly-fishing guide. He is happiest standing in a cold river patiently waiting for the next trout to bite. This recipe is his favorite way to prepare his catch. By grilling the fish in a foil packet, the trout steams in its own juices to create a moist and flavorful entrée.*

4 whole trout (about 10 to 12 ounces each), cleaned
Kosher salt and freshly ground black pepper
1 lemon, thinly sliced

4 cloves garlic, minced
1/4 cup thinly sliced white onions
1/2 cup freshly squeezed lemon juice
1/4 cup extra virgin olive oil

▶ Preheat a clean grill to medium-high with the lid closed for 8 to 10 minutes.

▶ Generously season the trout inside and out with the salt and pepper. Stuff the trout with the lemon slices, garlic, and onions. Place each trout on the center of a sheet of heavy-duty aluminum foil, about 18 inches square. Generously drizzle both sides of the trout with lemon juice and olive oil. Fold the foil over the fish and crimp the edges as tightly as possible to seal the packet.

▶ Place the aluminum foil packets on the grill. Close the lid and cook, turning the packets once, until the flesh is flaky and easily separates with a fork, about 7 minutes on each side. Serve immediately.

Serves 4.

 **Cooking Tips:** Grilling in aluminum foil packets is very similar to the French cooking technique *en papillote*, where ingredients are wrapped in parchment paper and baked. In addition to fish, this cooking technique is a delicious way to grill vegetables. Be sure to use heavy-duty aluminum foil, or double up on the regular kind.

Fresh herbs like thyme or oregano would be a delicious addition to this dish.

**Do-Ahead:** The foil packets can be made up to 3 hours in advance. Refrigerate until ready to cook.

**Suggested Side:** Smoky Steak Fries (page 191)

# Cedar Plank Salmon with Caper Remoulade

*This is one of my favorite ways to cook salmon. It's super easy, makes a great presentation, and the fish comes out deliciously smoky and moist.*

### For the Caper Remoulade:

1/4 cup mayonnaise

1/4 cup sour cream

2 tablespoons freshly squeezed lemon juice

4 tablespoons capers, drained

Kosher salt and freshly ground black pepper

### For the Cedar Plank Salmon:

4 4- to 6-ounce boneless salmon fillets

Kosher salt and freshly ground black pepper

1 cedar plank, soaked in water at least 4 hours and drained

▶ To make the Caper Remoulade: In a small bowl whisk together the mayonnaise, sour cream, and lemon juice. Stir in the capers. Season with the salt and pepper to taste. Cover and refrigerate until ready to serve.

▶ To make the Cedar Plank Salmon: Preheat a clean grill to medium-high with the lid closed for 8 to 10 minutes.

▶ Generously season the salmon with the salt and pepper. Place the salmon fillets on the cedar plank, skin side down.

▶ Place the plank in the center of the grill directly on the grates. Close the lid and cook until the fish is medium, about 10 to 12 minutes, or until desired doneness.

▶ To serve, place the fish on a plate and top with a generous spoonful of the remoulade sauce.

Serves 4.

**Cooking Tip:** Cedar planks are available at most grocery, kitchen supply, and hardware stores. When buying cedar planks at a hardware store, be sure to look for untreated wood.

**Do-Ahead:** The Caper Remoulade can be made the day before. Store covered in your refrigerator until ready to serve.

# Cedar Wrapped Mahi-Mahi with Mango and Red Peppers

*Folks have been using cedar planks to impart a smoky flavor to fish for years. Cedar papers allow you to steam a dish to perfection on the grill while a subtle smoky flavor is infused.*

1/4 cup orange juice
3 tablespoons freshly squeezed lime juice
2 tablespoons olive oil
4 4- to 6-ounce mahi-mahi fillets, cut into
    1-inch-thick slices
Vegetable oil, for the grates
4 cedar papers with cotton strings,
    soaked in water for 10 minutes

Kosher salt and freshly ground black
    pepper
2 mangos, pitted, peeled, and thinly sliced
1/4 cup thinly sliced red bell peppers
1/4 cup thinly sliced red onions
1 fresh jalapeño, thinly sliced

▸ In a small bowl whisk together the orange juice, lime juice, and olive oil until well combined. Place the mahi-mahi in a shallow nonreactive dish large enough to hold the fish in a single layer, and pour the marinade over the fish. Marinate for 10 minutes.

▸ Preheat a clean grill to medium-high with the lid closed for 8 to 10 minutes. Lightly brush the grates with oil.

▸ Place the soaked cedar papers on a work surface.

▸ Remove the fish from marinade, shake off the excess, and discard the marinade. Place 1/4 of the fish in the center of a soaked paper parallel to the grain of the wood. Season with the salt and pepper to taste. Repeat with the 3 remaining papers. Top with the mangos, red bell peppers, red onions, and jalapeno slices. Fold the edges of each paper over the fish and tie with a cotton string.

▸ Place the packets directly on the grill. Close the lid and cook, turning once, until medium, 4 to 5 minutes per side. To serve, place packets on dinner plates and allow your guests to unwrap.

Serves 4.

**Cooking Tip:** Since cedar papers are made from wood, they will burn if they are not soaked in a liquid for at least 10 minutes prior to grilling. The soaked papers add both moisture and a smoky cedar flavor to the dish. To add an extra depth of flavor, soak the cedar papers in orange juice, wine, or bourbon. Unfortunately, cedar papers can only be used once.

 **Suggested Side:** Grilled Asparagus (page 183)

# Hoisin-Glazed Sea Bass

*Hoisin sauce is often referred to as Chinese barbecue sauce. With the addition of ingredients like honey and ginger, this sweet yet spicy glaze is a delicious compliment to the richness of sea bass.*

1 tablespoon canola oil
2 cloves garlic, minced
1 teaspoon crushed red pepper flakes
1/2 cup hoisin sauce
1 tablespoon rice wine vinegar
1 tablespoon soy sauce
1 tablespoon honey

1 tablespoon freshly grated ginger
Vegetable oil, for the grates
4 4- to 6-ounce sea bass fillets
2 tablespoons olive oil
Kosher salt and freshly ground black
    pepper

▶ In a small saucepan over medium heat, warm the canola oil. Add the garlic and red pepper flakes, and sauté until just fragrant. Do not brown. Reduce the heat to low and whisk in the hoisin sauce, vinegar, soy sauce, honey, and ginger until warmed and well combined. Cook until warmed through, about 3 to 5 minutes. Remove from the heat and cover to keep warm until ready to brush on the fish.

▶ Preheat a clean grill to medium-high with the lid closed for 8 to 10 minutes. Lightly brush the grates with oil.

▶ Brush the sea bass fillets with the olive oil. Season with the salt and pepper to taste.

▶ Place sea bass on the grill, close the lid, and cook until golden brown, about 4 minutes. Turn over and brush with the glaze. Continue cooking until medium, another 4 minutes.

▶ To serve, place the fish on the plate and brush with the additional glaze.

Serves 4.

**Do-Ahead:** The hoisin glaze can be made 1 day in advance. Store covered in your refrigerator until ready to serve. Warm over low heat before using.

**Suggested Side:** Miso Eggplant (page 197)

# New Orleans–Style Barbecue Shrimp

*While most places prepare their New Orleans–style barbecue shrimp in a cast-iron skillet, I like the smoky flavor that a grill adds to this rendition.*

2 pounds large shrimp, deveined and in the shell

1/4 cup Creole seasoning

3 tablespoons olive oil

8 tablespoons (1 stick) plus 1 tablespoon unsalted butter, divided

2 cloves garlic, minced

1 tablespoon Worcestershire sauce

1 tablespoon freshly squeezed lemon juice

1 tablespoon freshly ground black pepper

1/2 cup dry white wine

Vegetable oil, for the grates

Crusty French bread (optional)

▶ In a large nonreactive bowl, toss the shrimp with the Creole seasoning and the olive oil. Cover and refrigerate for at least 30 minutes or up to 1 hour.

▶ In a medium sauté pan over medium-high heat, melt 1 tablespoon of the butter. Add the garlic and sauté until just fragrant; do not brown. Add the Worcestershire sauce, lemon juice, and pepper. Add the white wine and stir to deglaze the sauté pan. Cook until the sauce is reduced by half.

▶ Reduce the heat to medium-low and add the remaining butter 1 tablespoon at a time, mixing until completely incorporated after each addition and cooking until the sauce is thickened enough to coat a spoon. Keep warm over low heat.

▶ Preheat a clean grill with a grill basket or screen to medium with the lid closed for 8 to 10 minutes. Lightly oil the grill basket or screen.

▶ Place the shrimp in a single layer on the grill basket or screen. Close the lid and cook, turning once, until the shrimp turn pink, about 2 to 3 minutes per side.

▶ Transfer the shrimp to a large bowl. Pour the warm sauce over the top and toss to coat. Serve warm with crusty French bread if desired.

Serves 4.

**Cooking Tips:** If you would like to make your own Creole seasoning, it's really not hard to do. Just whisk together 1/4 cup paprika and 1/2 teaspoon each of dried thyme, dried oregano, cayenne pepper, garlic powder, onion powder, salt, and black pepper. This mixture will store for several weeks, tightly sealed, in your spice cabinet.

If you don't have a grill basket or screen, you can cook the shrimp on skewers to prevent them falling through the grates. Just be sure to soak bamboo skewers for 30 minutes before you grill.

**M Marinate:** At least 30 minutes but not more than 1 hour.

# Lemon-Rosemary Scallops

*The rosemary sprigs not only make a dramatic presentation for this dish, but they also add flavor to the scallops.*

12 large sea scallops, about 2 to 2 1/2
    pounds
1/4 cup dry white wine
4 tablespoons freshly squeezed lemon
    juice
1 tablespoon olive oil

Vegetable oil, for the grates
Kosher salt and freshly ground black
    pepper
12 fresh rosemary sprigs, soaked in water
    for 30 minutes and drained

▶ Rinse the scallops and pat dry. Place the scallops in a shallow nonreactive dish.

▶ In a small bowl, whisk together the white wine, lemon juice, and olive oil until well blended. Pour the marinade over the scallops and toss to coat. Marinate for 5 to 10 minutes.

▶ Preheat a clean grill to medium-high with the lid closed for 8 to 10 minutes. Lightly brush the grates with oil.

▶ Remove the scallops from the marinade, shake off any excess, and discard the marinade. Season the scallops with the salt and pepper to taste. Slide a scallop onto each of the rosemary sprigs.

▶ Grill on one side until the scallops develop golden brown grill marks, about 2 to 3 minutes. Turn over and continue cooking until the interior just starts to turn opaque, another 2 to 3 minutes. Serve immediately.

Serves 4.

**Cooking Tips:** Always place the skewer through the center of the scallop lengthwise rather than through the top, or the scallop may break.
    Don't like the flavor of rosemary? Just use soaked bamboo skewers or metal skewers instead.

**Variation:** This marinade would be delicious on other white fish such as tilapia, mahi-mahi, or even squid.

**Marinate:** 5 to 10 minutes. Do not marinate the scallops for longer than 10 minutes. The acid in the lemon juice will begin to "cook" and toughen this delicate shellfish if it is left to marinate for any longer.

# Honey Mustard Salmon

*Jazz up a piece of grilled salmon with tangy yet sweet Honey Dijon mustard.*

Vegetable oil, for the grates
4 4- to 6-ounce boneless salmon fillets
2 tablespoons olive oil

Kosher salt and freshly ground black
   pepper
1/2 cup Honey Dijon mustard

▸ Preheat a clean grill to medium-high with the lid closed for 8 to 10 minutes. Lightly brush the grates with oil.

▸ Brush the salmon with the olive oil. Season with the salt and pepper to taste.

▸ Place salmon on the grill, flesh side down. Close the lid and cook for about 3 to 4 minutes. Turn the salmon over and brush with the mustard. Cook for 3 to 5 more minutes, for medium. Serve immediately.

Serves 4.

**Cooking Tips:** The secret to grilling salmon (or any fish) is to let a good crust form on the outside before you try to flip it. If you try to flip it before it is ready, the flesh will tear and fall apart.

    There are many great brands of Honey Dijon mustard available. One of my favorites is made by French's®. If you don't have a bottle on hand, you can make your own by combining equal parts honey and Dijon mustard.

# Grouper Tacos with Jalapeno-Lime Slaw

*I often find inspiration in the kitchen based on memories. This fish taco reminds me of a trip to the Bahamas where I enjoyed a delicious taco filled with just-caught grouper and a citrusy slaw.*

### For the Jalapeno-Lime Slaw:

1/4 cup mayonnaise
3 tablespoons freshly squeezed lime juice
2 cups finely shredded green cabbage
1 cup finely shredded red cabbage
1/4 cup thinly sliced red onions (about half a small onion)
2 tablespoons seeded and finely diced fresh jalapenos
2 tablespoons coarsely chopped fresh cilantro
Kosher salt and freshly ground black pepper

### For the Grouper Tacos:

1/4 cup freshly squeezed lime juice
3 tablespoons olive oil
1 clove garlic, minced
1 teaspoon chili powder
1/2 teaspoon cumin
4 6-ounce grouper fillets
Vegetable oil, for the grates
Kosher salt and freshly ground black pepper
8 small (4-inch) flour tortillas, warmed
2 avocados, halved, seeded, peeled, and sliced

▶ To make the Jalapeno-Lime Slaw: In a large mixing bowl, whisk together the mayonnaise and lime juice. Add the green cabbage, red cabbage, red onions, jalapenos, and cilantro. Toss until well combined. Season with the salt and pepper to taste. Cover and refrigerate until ready to serve.

▶ To make the Grouper Tacos: In small bowl whisk together the lime juice, olive oil, garlic, chili powder, and cumin until well blended. Place the grouper in a shallow nonreactive dish large enough to hold the fish in a single layer, and pour the marinade over the fish. Cover and refrigerate for at least 30 minutes or up to 1 hour.

▶ Preheat a clean grill to medium-high with the lid closed for 8 to 10 minutes. Lightly brush the grates with oil.

▶ Remove the fish from the marinade, shake off any excess, and discard the marinade. Season both sides of the fish with the salt and pepper to taste.

▶ Place the grouper on the grill. Close the lid and cook, turning once, until medium, 4 to 5 minutes per side.

▶ Assemble the tacos by placing the fish (approximately half a fillet per taco) in the center of the tortillas. Garnish with slices of avocado and a spoonful of the slaw. Serve warm.

Serves 4.

**Cooking Tips:** These tacos can easily be made with any firm-fleshed white fish, such as halibut, snapper, mahi-mahi, or cod.
    Do not marinate the fish longer than 1 hour. The acid in the lime juice will start to "cook" the fish and cause it to be tough.

**(M) Marinate:** At least 30 minutes or up to 1 hour.

# Grilled Tuna with Orange and Fennel Slaw

*This is my rendition of a dish I had years ago at a restaurant in Spain. The sweet and savory slaw is the perfect accompaniment to a perfectly seared piece of tuna.*

### For the Orange and Fennel Slaw:
- 1/4 cup orange juice
- 1 tablespoon Dijon mustard
- 1 tablespoon olive oil
- 3 oranges, peeled and segmented
- 1 fennel bulb, trimmed, cored, and thinly sliced lengthwise
- 1/2 cup pitted green Spanish olives
- 1/4 cup thinly sliced red onions
- 3 tablespoons chopped fresh mint leaves
- Pinch of crushed red pepper flakes
- Kosher salt and freshly ground black pepper

### For the Grilled Tuna:
- Vegetable oil, for the grates
- 4 6-ounce fresh tuna steaks, each about 1-inch thick
- 2 tablespoons olive oil
- Kosher salt and freshly ground black pepper

▶ To make the Orange and Fennel Slaw: In a small bowl, whisk together the orange juice, mustard, and olive oil. In a large bowl place the orange segments, fennel, olives, onions, mint, and red pepper flakes. Add the dressing and toss to combine. Season with the salt and pepper to taste. Cover and refrigerate until ready to serve.

▶ To make the Grilled Tuna: Preheat a clean grill to medium-high with the lid closed for 8 to 10 minutes. Lightly brush the grates with oil.

▶ Brush both sides of the tuna with olive oil. Generously season with the salt and pepper.

▶ Place the tuna on the grill. Cook, turning once, until just seared on the outside and still rare on the inside, about 3 minutes per side.

▶ To serve, place the tuna on the plate and top with a generous spoonful of the slaw.

Serves 4.

**Cooking Tips:** To trim and core a bulb of fennel, first cut off the stalks from the top of the bulb and remove any tough outer layers. Then cut the bulb into quarters and remove the hard core with a paring knife.

Tuna steaks are traditionally served rare. If you prefer a more done piece of fish, just cook until your desired temperature is reached.

# Grilled Tilapia with Lemon and Caper Sauce

*Think Piccata meets fish! Brown butter is one of my signature cooking "tricks." I use it to season vegetables, as a sauce for fish, and have even drizzled it into cake batter. By adding capers and lemon to the mix, the sauce for this dish is very similar to the one in a classic veal piccata.*

### For the Grilled Tilapia:
Vegetable oil, for the grates
4 6-ounce tilapia fillets
2 tablespoons olive oil
Kosher salt and freshly ground black
  pepper
1 lemon, thinly sliced into rounds

### For the Lemon and Caper Sauce:
6 tablespoons unsalted butter
3 tablespoons drained capers

▶ To make the Grilled Tilapia: Preheat a clean grill to medium-high with the lid closed for 8 to 10 minutes. Lightly brush the grates with oil.

▶ Brush the tilapia fillets with the olive oil. Season with the salt and pepper to taste.

▶ Place the tilapia on the grill. Close the lid and cook, turning once, until medium, about 4 minutes per side. Place the lemon slices on the grill and cook until grill marks appear, about 1 minute per side.

▶ To make the Lemon and Caper Sauce: Place the butter in a medium saucepan. Over medium-high heat, cook, swirling the pot occasionally, until the butter stops foaming and begins to brown. Remove from the heat. Stir in the capers and grilled lemon slices.

▶ To serve, place the fish on a plate and top with a generous spoonful of the sauce, being sure to evenly distribute the capers and lemon slices. Serve immediately.

Serves 4.

**Cooking Tip:** By slightly browning the butter, you give it a delicious nutty flavor. Be careful though: this sauce is ready the moment it starts to brown. If you overcook it, it will taste burnt.

**Variation:** Other flaky white fish, like red snapper or sole, would be delicious with this sauce.

**Suggested Side:** Grilled Asparagus (page 183)

# Grilled Lobster Tails with Drawn Butter

*You will be shocked at how simple lobster is to grill. I like the convenience of using lobster tails, but if you are adventurous, you can grill a whole lobster too.*

### For the Drawn Butter:
1 cup unsalted butter (2 sticks), at room
     temperature

### For the Grilled Lobster:
Vegetable oil, for the grates
Kosher salt
8 8-ounce lobster tails in the shell
4 tablespoons olive oil
Kosher salt and freshly ground black
     pepper

▸ To make the Drawn Butter: In a small saucepan, melt the butter over medium-low heat until the milk solids have separated and sunk to the bottom of the pan. Ladle out the clarified butter leaving behind the solids on the bottom. Cover the drawn butter to keep warm until the lobster is done. Discard the milk solids.

▸ To make the Grilled Lobster: Preheat a clean grill to medium-high with the lid closed for 8 to 10 minutes. Lightly brush the grates with oil.

▸ Bring a large pot of salted water to boil over high heat. Add the lobster tails and boil for 6 minutes. Transfer the lobsters to a cutting board.

▸ Butterfly each lobster tail lengthwise down the underside with kitchen shears or a heavy knife, taking care not to cut through the back shell so that the lobster is still in one piece. Spread the halves of the tails so that the meat is exposed. Brush the flesh side of each lobster tail with the oil, and season with the salt and pepper to taste.

▸ Place the lobster on the grill with the flesh side down. Close the lid and cook, turning once, until slightly charred, about 3 to 4 minutes per side.

▸ Serve with a ramekin of the drawn butter on the side for dipping.

Serves 4.

**Suggested Side:** Grilled Corn on the Cob (page 199) garnished simply with extra drawn butter.

# Grilled Halibut with Cherry Tomato Salad

*Sometimes simplicity is best. I like to serve this simple grilled fish dish in the summertime when just-picked tomatoes and basil taste so good they only need a drizzle of olive oil and balsamic vinegar to dress them up.*

### For the Cherry Tomato Salad:
2 cups cherry tomatoes, halved
1/4 cup finely diced red onions
1 clove garlic, minced
1 tablespoon olive oil
2 tablespoons balsamic vinegar
1/3 cup thinly sliced fresh basil
Kosher salt and freshly ground pepper

### For the Grilled Halibut:
Vegetable oil, for the grates
4 4- to 6-ounce halibut fillets
2 tablespoons olive oil
Kosher salt and freshly ground black pepper

▸ To make the Cherry Tomato Salad: Place the tomatoes, onions, garlic, olive oil, balsamic vinegar, and basil in a medium bowl. Toss to combine. Season with the salt and pepper to taste.

▸ To make the Grilled Halibut: Preheat a clean grill to medium-high with the lid closed for 8 to 10 minutes. Lightly brush the grates with oil.

▸ Brush the halibut fillets with the olive oil. Season with the salt and pepper to taste.

▸ Place the fillets on the grill. Close the lid and cook, turning once, until medium, about 4 minutes per side.

▸ To serve, place the fish on a plate and top with a generous spoonful of the tomato salad.

Serves 4.

**Cooking Tip:** Basil has a tendency to blacken once it is cut. To keep it from darkening, chop and add the basil just before serving.

**Do-Ahead:** The tomato salad can be made 4 hours ahead. Store covered in your refrigerator until ready to serve.

# Fire-Roasted Mussels

*This classic French preparation of mussels with white wine works beautifully on the grill. Be sure to serve it with crusty bread because everyone will want to sop up all the scrumptious sauce.*

8 tablespoons (1 stick) unsalted butter
2 shallots, peeled and thinly sliced
4 cloves garlic, minced
4 sprigs of fresh thyme

1 cup dry white wine
2 pounds mussels, well rinsed

▶ Preheat a clean grill to medium-high with the lid closed for 8 to 10 minutes.

▶ Place a cast-iron Dutch oven in the center of the grill. Add the butter and melt with the lid closed, about 2 minutes. Add the shallots, garlic, and thyme. Sauté until softened, about 3 to 5 minutes. Add the wine and stir to combine.

▶ Add the mussels, stir gently, and close the lid. Cook for 4 to 5 minutes, or until the mussels open.

▶ Serve immediately.

Serves 6.

**Cooking Tips:** To prepare the mussels, first discard any with broken shells or any that are open. Rinse under cold water to remove any dirt or the "beard" near the hinge.

I find that a cast-iron Dutch oven works well for this dish because it can stand up to the heat of the grill. If you don't have one, you can prepare this dish in an aluminum tray. Place the mussels in the tray, prepare the sauce indoors in a stock pot, and pour the sauce over the mussels. Then place the mussels on the grill to cook.

# Salads

I love salads. And not surprisingly, I have written a cookbook on them as well as designed two restaurant concepts based on this dish.

*Simply Salads* was inspired by my favorite lunchtime dish. As I developed recipes for that book, I experienced firsthand that the possibilities are infinite when it comes to the different salad creations you can make. It's fun to experiment with flavors.

Cheffie's Café is my newest restaurant venture. I designed a concept and a menu around fresh salads and sandwiches. At Cheffie's Café, we invite our guests to "Be the Chef." From our long list of top-quality meats, fresh produce, tasty cheeses, and delicious toppings, guests can design their own salad or sandwich creation. We want our guests to have fun composing their personal salads.

Salads take very little time to prepare and are impossible to mess up. You can make a salad with just about any food. It's as simple as tossing together a handful of fresh, flavorful ingredients. There really are no rules.

Depending on what you decide to toss together, salads can either be tasty sides or satisfying entrées. I have included both options in this chapter. A grill can add a delicious, smoky flavor to just about everything. From corn (page 199) and summer squashes (page 187) to romaine lettuce (page 147) and potatoes (page 149)!

# Asparagus and Cherry Tomato Salad

*This was one of my most popular salads at my prepared foods market, Cheffie's Market & More. The combination of asparagus, cherry tomatoes, tangy vinaigrette, and salty capers is absolutely delicious.*

Vegetable oil, for the grates
1 bunch (about 1 pound) asparagus, tough woody ends snapped off and discarded
5 tablespoons olive oil, divided
Kosher salt and freshly ground black pepper
1 pint cherry tomatoes, cut into quarters

1/4 cup finely diced red onions (1/2 small onion)
3 tablespoons capers, drained
2 cloves garlic, minced
2 tablespoons red wine vinegar
1 tablespoon freshly squeezed lemon juice

▶ Preheat a clean grill to medium-high with the lid closed for 8 to 10 minutes. Lightly brush the grates with oil.

▶ Place the asparagus on a baking sheet. Drizzle with 2 tablespoons of the olive oil and toss until well coated. Season with the salt and pepper to taste.

▶ Place the asparagus on the grill. Cook, turning once or twice, until tender and slightly charred, about 3 to 5 minutes on each side.

Remove from the grill and let cool to room temperature.

▶ Cut the stalks into 1 1/2-inch pieces and place in a large bowl. Add the tomatoes, onions, capers, garlic, vinegar, lemon juice, and the remaining olive oil. Toss until well combined. Season with salt and pepper to taste. Serve at room temperature or chilled.

Serves 6.

✔ **Do-Ahead:** The asparagus can be grilled in advance and chilled until you are ready to prepare the salad.

# Cashew Noodle Salad with Miso-Ginger Tofu Skewers

*Justin Fox Burks not only takes stunning photos of food, but he also creates mouthwatering vegetarian dishes like this one for his blog, The Chubby Vegetarian.*

## For the Cashew Noodle Salad:
- 1 cup cashews
- 1/4 cup soy sauce
- 2 tablespoons sambal chili paste
- 1/4 cup sesame oil
- 1/4 cup mirin
- 1/4 cup rice vinegar
- 1 clove garlic, minced
- 1/2 pound spaghetti or soba noodles, cooked per package directions and cooled
- 1/4 cup thinly sliced scallions

## For the Miso-Ginger Tofu Skewers:
- 1 tablespoon red miso
- 1 tablespoon soy sauce
- 1/2 teaspoon sesame oil
- 2 tablespoons rice vinegar
- 3 tablespoons mirin
- 1 tablespoon finely grated fresh ginger
- 2 cloves garlic, minced
- 1 teaspoon sugar
- 2 tablespoons water
- Dash of sriracha or your favorite hot sauce
- 1 block (14-ounce) extra-firm tofu, cut into 1-inch cubes
- Vegetable oil, for the grates
- Skewers (if using bamboo, soak in water for 30 minutes)
- Cornstarch, for dusting

▶ To make the Cashew Noodle Salad: Place the cashews, soy sauce, sambal, sesame oil, mirin, rice vinegar, and garlic into a food processor and pulse until smooth. Place the noodles in a large bowl. Add the cashew sauce and sliced scallions. Toss until well coated. Refrigerate until ready to serve.

▶ To make the Miso-Ginger Tofu Skewers: In a shallow nonreactive dish just large enough to hold the tofu in a single layer, stir together the miso, soy sauce, sesame oil, rice vinegar, mirin, ginger, garlic, sugar, water, and sriracha. Place the tofu in the marinade and gently toss until well coated. Cover, refrigerate, and marinate for at least 1 hour or as long as overnight.

▶ Preheat a clean grill to medium-high with the lid closed for 8 to 10 minutes. Lightly brush the grates with oil.

▶ Remove the tofu from the marinade. Shake off the excess and pat dry. Thread the tofu onto the skewers. Lightly dust with the cornstarch.

▶ Strain the marinade into a small pot over medium-high heat. Allow mixture to reduce by half or until slightly thickened.

▶ Place the tofu on the grill. Close the lid and cook until golden brown, about 4 minutes. Turn over and lightly brush with the reduced marinade. Cook an additional 4 minutes.

Remove from the grill and brush again with the marinade.

▶ To serve, place the tofu skewers on top of the cashew noodle salad.

Serves 4.

 **Cooking Tips:** Lightly dusting the tofu skewers on both sides with cornstarch will help prevent sticking and allow the reduced marinade to cling to the tofu.

Sriracha and sambal are both fiery condiments from southeast Asia. Sriracha is a Thai hot sauce made with chile peppers, garlic, vinegar, sugar, and salt. It is mostly used as a condiment or dipping sauce. Sambal is of Indonesian and Malaysian origin. It is made from a variety of different chiles, usually a pepper like cayenne. Use sambal when you want to add heat without impacting the flavor of the dish. It's not really used so much as a condiment as it is used for cooking. You will find both of these condiments at an Asian food market or in the international aisle at your grocery store.

 **Do-Ahead:** The Cashew Noodle Salad will last up to a week covered and refrigerated. In fact, it is one of those dishes that some say tastes even better the second day.

# Grilled Chicken Salad with Asparagus and Blue Cheese

*This is my fun twist on chicken salad. Colorful and flavorful, it's a one-dish meal that's my go-to when I need to make lunch for a group.*

4 boneless, skinless chicken breasts
    (about 1 1/2 pounds)
5 tablespoons olive oil, divided
6 tablespoons Dijon mustard, divided
1 bunch (about 1 pound) asparagus, tough
    woody ends snapped off and
    discarded
1/2 cup thinly sliced red onions (1 small onion)

1/2 cup thinly sliced red bell peppers
    (1 small pepper)
1/2 cup thinly sliced yellow bell peppers
    (1 small pepper)
Vegetable oil, for the grates
Kosher salt and freshly ground black pepper
1/2 cup crumbled blue cheese or
    Gorgonzola

▸ In a shallow nonreactive dish just large enough to hold the chicken in a single layer, stir together 2 tablespoons of the olive oil and 4 tablespoons of the mustard. Add the chicken and toss to coat. Cover, refrigerate, and marinate for 30 minutes.

▸ While the chicken is marinating, prepare the vegetables. Cut the asparagus into 2-inch pieces. Over high heat, bring a medium pot of salted water to a boil. Add the asparagus and cook until vibrant green and crisp tender, 1 to 1 1/2 minutes. Drain the asparagus and rinse with cold water to cool. Reserve.

▸ In a large skillet over medium-high heat, warm 1 tablespoon of the olive oil until a few droplets of water sizzle when carefully sprinkled in the pan. Add the onions, red bell peppers, and yellow bell peppers. Cook, stirring frequently, until the vegetables are soft, about 5 minutes. Refrigerate to cool.

▸ Heat a clean grill to medium-high with the lid closed for 8 to 10 minutes. Lightly brush the grates with oil.

▸ Generously season the marinated chicken with the salt and pepper. Place the chicken on the grill. Close the lid and cook, turning once, until no longer pink in the middle, 6 to 8 minutes per side. Remove the chicken from the grill and let it rest for 5 minutes. Slice thinly against the grain. Refrigerate until cool.

▸ In a large bowl, toss the chicken with the asparagus, red onions, red bell peppers, and yellow bell peppers. Add the remaining 2 tablespoons of oil and 2 tablespoons mustard and toss to coat. Add the crumbled blue cheese and toss. Season with salt and pepper to taste. Serve chilled or at room temperature.

Serves 4 to 6.

**Cooking Tip:** I prefer to sauté the peppers and onions individually so that they keep their vibrant colors.

**Marinate:** 30 minutes.

# Grilled Shrimp with Cucumber and Heirloom Tomato Salad

*Midsummer my garden is overflowing with tomatoes and cucumbers. For a refreshing but satisfying meal, I add grilled shrimp to a colorful salad made from my favorite summer produce.*

### For the Grilled Shrimp:

Vegetable oil, for the grates
1 1/2 pounds medium-large shrimp (16-20 count), peeled and deveined
2 tablespoons olive oil
Kosher salt and freshly ground black pepper

### For the Cucumber and Heirloom Tomato Salad:

4 small cucumbers, sliced into 1/4-inch rounds
4 heirloom tomatoes, cored and cut into 1/4-inch wedges
1/4 cup thinly sliced Vidalia onions
1/4 cup red wine vinegar
2 tablespoons olive oil
1/4 cup chopped fresh basil
Kosher salt and freshly ground black pepper

▶ To make the Grilled Shrimp: Preheat a clean grill with a grill screen or basket to medium-high with the lid closed for 8 to 10 minutes. Lightly brush the grill screen or basket with oil.

▶ Place the shrimp and olive oil in a large bowl and toss to coat. Generously season with the salt and pepper.

▶ Place the shrimp on the grill screen or basket in a single layer. Close the lid and cook, turning once, until they turn pink, about 2 to 3 minutes per side. Remove from the grill and set aside.

▶ To make the Cucumber and Heirloom Tomato Salad: Place the cucumbers, tomatoes, and onions in a large bowl. Add the vinegar, olive oil, and basil and gently toss to combine. Season with the salt and pepper to taste.

▶ Add the shrimp just before serving and gently toss. Serve immediately.

Serves 4.

**Cooking Tip:** If you can't find heirloom tomatoes near you, this salad would also be delicious with any ripe tomato from the garden or market.

**V** **Variation:** Omit the shrimp for a refreshing summer side salad.

# Tuna Nicoise Salad with Lemon-Caper Vinaigrette

*Tuna Nicoise is a classic French dish that finds its origins in Nice, a town in southern France. It's one of my favorite main course salads.*

### For the Lemon-Caper Vinaigrette:
2 tablespoons freshly squeezed lemon juice
1 tablespoon Dijon mustard
6 tablespoons olive oil
2 tablespoons capers
Freshly ground black pepper

### For the Tuna Nicoise Salad:
Vegetable oil, for the grates
4 6-ounce fresh tuna steaks, each about
    1-inch thick
2 tablespoons olive oil

Kosher salt and freshly ground black pepper
1 large head butter lettuce, leaves
    separated and torn into 1-inch pieces
8 small red new potatoes, boiled until
    tender, cooled, and cut in quarters
1/4 pound haricots verts, trimmed, boiled
    until crisp-tender, and cooled
4 hard-boiled eggs, peeled and quartered
1 cup halved cherry tomatoes
1/2 cup pitted Nicoise or kalamata olives
1/4 cup thinly sliced red onions (about 1/2
    small onion)

▶ To make the Lemon-Caper Vinaigrette: In a small bowl whisk together the lemon juice and mustard. Slowly add the olive oil in a stream, whisking to emulsify. Stir in the capers. Season with the pepper to taste. Cover and refrigerate until ready to serve.

▶ To make the Tuna Nicoise Salad: Preheat a clean grill to medium-high with the lid closed for 8 to 10 minutes. Lightly brush the grates with oil.

▶ Brush both sides of the tuna with olive oil. Generously season with the salt and pepper.

▶ Place the tuna on the grill. Cook, turning once, until just seared on the outside and still rare on the inside, about 3 minutes per side. Place the tuna on a cutting board and thinly slice.

▶ On a plate arrange the lettuce, potatoes, haricots verts, eggs, tomatoes, olives, and onions. Top with the tuna slices. Drizzle with the vinaigrette to taste. Serve immediately.

Serves 4.

 **Cooking Tips:** Haricots verts are tender, skinny French green beans. Many grocery stores now carry them in either the fresh or the frozen vegetable section. If you can't find them, just use traditional fresh green beans.
    Tuna steaks are traditionally served rare. If you prefer a more done piece of fish, just cook to your desired temperature.

 **Do-Ahead:** To save some time, you can cook the potatoes and haricots verts ahead. Cool and refrigerate until ready to toss all the ingredients.

**Ⓥ Variation:** Salmon would be a delicious substitute for the tuna in this salad.

# Panzanella Salad

*Originally invented by the Italians as a way to use up day-old bread, this salad is delicious no matter how old—or not—the bread is.*

### For the Croutons:

Vegetable oil, for the grates
1/2 small loaf (15-ounce) French or Italian
    country bread, sliced 1-inch thick
2 tablespoons olive oil
Kosher salt and freshly ground black
    pepper

### For the Red Wine–Garlic Vinaigrette:

1 clove garlic, minced
2 tablespoons red wine vinegar
6 tablespoons olive oil
Kosher salt and freshly ground black
    pepper

### For the Salad:

1 large tomato, cut into 1-inch pieces
1 small cucumber, halved, seeded, and
    cut into 1/2-inch pieces
1 cup diced red bell peppers (1 large
    pepper)
1 cup diced yellow bell peppers (1 large
    pepper)
1/2 cup thinly sliced red onions (1 small
    onion)
10 large basil leaves, sliced into thin strips

▶ For the Croutons: Preheat a clean grill to medium-high with the lid closed for 8 to 10 minutes. Lightly brush the grates with oil.

▶ Brush the bread with the olive oil and season with the salt and pepper. Grill on both sides until golden brown, about 2 minutes per side. Remove from the grill and cut each slice into 1-inch cubes.

▶ For the Red Wine–Garlic Vinaigrette: In a small bowl whisk together the garlic and vinegar. Slowly add the olive oil in a steady stream, whisking to emulsify. Season with the salt and pepper to taste. Cover and refrigerate until ready to serve.

▶ For the Salad: In a large salad bowl, toss together the tomatoes, cucumbers, red bell peppers, yellow bell peppers, onions, and basil. Add the croutons and the vinaigrette to taste. Toss gently. Set aside to allow the croutons to soak up the vinaigrette, 10 to 20 minutes before serving.

Serves 4 to 6.

**Cooking Tip:** A quick trick to cut basil into thin strips, also known as a chiffonade, is to place clean leaves in a pile, roll the leaves lengthwise like a cigarette, and thinly slice the roll crosswise.

# Mediterranean Quinoa Salad

*Quinoa is a high-protein, gluten-free grain that cooks much like rice and has a texture similar to couscous. It makes a delicious and healthy base for a salad.*

Vegetable oil, for the grill basket or screen
1 red onion, cut into 1/2-inch slices
1 small eggplant, cut into 1-inch cubes
1 red bell pepper, cut into 1-inch squares
1 zucchini, cut lengthwise and then into 1/2-inch slices
1/4 cup plus 2 tablespoons olive oil, divided
Kosher salt and freshly ground black pepper

2 cups cooked quinoa, prepared per package directions
1 tablespoon red wine vinegar
1 tablespoon freshly squeezed lemon juice
1 clove garlic, minced
1 teaspoon crushed red pepper flakes
1/4 cup finely chopped fresh cilantro

▶ Preheat a clean grill with a grill basket or screen to medium-high with the lid closed for 8 to 10 minutes. Lightly brush the grill basket or screen with oil.

▶ In a large bowl toss together the onions, eggplant, red bell peppers, zucchini, and 1/4 cup of the olive oil. Season with the salt and pepper to taste.

▶ Transfer the vegetables to the grill basket. Close the lid and cook, turning once or twice, until the vegetables are tender and slightly charred, about 5 to 7 minutes per side.

▶ Place the prepared quinoa in a large bowl. Add the grilled vegetables and toss to combine.

▶ In a small bowl whisk together the remaining 2 tablespoons olive oil, red wine vinegar, lemon juice, garlic, and red pepper flakes. Pour the dressing over the salad and toss to coat. Season with salt and pepper to taste. Garnish with the cilantro. Serve warm or chilled.

Serves 4.

**Do-Ahead:** The quinoa can be made a day ahead. Store covered in the refrigerator until ready to use.

# Grilled Caesar Salad

*Slightly grilling the romaine gives it an unforgettably delicious smoky flavor. To make this a main course, add grilled chicken or shrimp.*

### For the Caesar Dressing:

2 cloves garlic, minced
2 anchovy fillets, minced, or 1/2 teaspoon anchovy paste
1 egg
2 tablespoons freshly squeezed lemon juice
1 tablespoon Dijon mustard
1/4 teaspoon Worcestershire sauce
1/2 cup olive oil
Kosher salt and freshly ground pepper

### For the Salad:

Vegetable oil, for the grates
1/2 small loaf (15-ounce) French or Italian country bread, sliced 1-inch thick
4 tablespoons olive oil, divided
Kosher salt and freshly ground black pepper
2 heads hearts of romaine, rinsed and patted dry
1/2 cup shredded Parmesan

▶ To make the Caesar Dressing: In a small bowl whisk together the garlic, anchovies, egg, lemon juice, mustard, and Worcestershire sauce. Add the olive oil in a stream, whisking until the dressing is emulsified. Season with the salt and pepper to taste. Refrigerate until ready to serve.

▶ To make the Salad: Preheat a clean grill to medium with the lid closed for 8 to 10 minutes. Lightly brush the grates with oil.

▶ Brush the bread with 2 tablespoons of the olive oil and season with the salt and pepper. Grill on both sides until golden brown, about 2 minutes per side. Remove from the grill and cut each slice into 1-inch cubes.

▶ Cut the romaine hearts in half lengthwise so that the stem keeps each piece together. Brush the romaine with the remaining 2 tablespoons of the olive oil and season with the salt and pepper to taste.

▶ Place the romaine on the grill, cut-side down. Close the lid and cook, turning frequently, until slightly charred but not heated all the way through, about 5 minutes total.

▶ Place one wedge on each plate. Generously drizzle with the dressing. Top with the croutons and Parmesan. Garnish with freshly ground pepper if desired. Serve immediately.

Serves 4.

**Cooking Tip:** Because it has a raw egg in it, this dressing must be refrigerated and used the same day it is made. If you are wary of serving a dressing with raw egg, substitute 1 tablespoon mayonnaise for the egg.

# Grilled Potato Salad

*Picnic-friendly grilled potato salad is a tasty twist on this traditional summer side.*

2 pounds small red potatoes
Kosher salt
Vegetable oil, for the grill screen
1/4 cup plus 3 tablespoons olive oil,
    divided
Kosher salt and freshly ground black
    pepper

1/2 cup thinly sliced roasted red bell
    peppers
1/4 cup thinly sliced red onions (about 1/2
    small onion)
2 tablespoons whole-grain mustard
1 tablespoon white wine vinegar

▶ Put the potatoes in a large pot and cover with cold salted water. Bring to a boil over high heat and then lower the temperature to a simmer. Cook just until they are tender but still firm, about 10 to 12 minutes. Drain and pat dry. Cut into 1-inch pieces and place in a large bowl.

▶ Preheat a clean grill with a grill screen to medium-high with the lid closed for 8 to 10 minutes. Lightly brush the grill screen with oil.

▶ Toss the potatoes with 1/4 cup of the olive oil until evenly coated. Season with the salt and pepper to taste.

▶ Place the potatoes on the grill. Close the lid and cook, turning occasionally, until browned on all sides and cooked through, about 8 to 10 minutes total.

▶ Place the potatoes in a large bowl. Add the roasted red bell peppers and red onions. Toss to combine. In a small bowl whisk together the mustard, vinegar, and remaining 3 tablespoons olive oil. Add to the potato salad and toss until well coated. Season with salt and pepper to taste. Serve warm or chilled.

Serves 4 to 6.

**Cooking Tips:** Be sure to reduce the temperature of the water right when it comes to a boil. You want to cook the potatoes at a gentle simmer so that they do not break.

Boiling the potatoes before grilling ensures that you will have potatoes with a nice crispy crust with a soft-done interior.

# Grilled Corn and Green Bean Salad

*This easy summer side dish is a great addition to any backyard barbecue. I like to make this colorful and chilled side dish ahead of time so I am free to enjoy time with my guests.*

Vegetable oil, for the grates
4 ears fresh corn, shucked
2 tablespoons unsalted butter, softened
Kosher salt and freshly ground black
    pepper
1 pound green beans, trimmed, boiled
    until crisp-tender, and cooled
1 1/2 cups halved cherry tomatoes

1/4 cup thinly sliced red onions (1/2 small
    onion)
1 teaspoon Dijon mustard
3 tablespoons red wine vinegar
1/4 cup olive oil
1/4 cup crumbled goat cheese

▸ Preheat a clean grill to medium-high with the lid closed for 8 to 10 minutes. Lightly brush the grates with oil.

▸ Brush the corn with the butter. Season with the salt and pepper to taste.

▸ Place the corn on the grill. Close the lid and cook, turning occasionally, until just tender and slightly charred on all sides, 8 to 10 minutes total. Transfer the corn to a cutting board to cool.

▸ When the corn is cool enough to handle, use a sharp knife to carefully slice the kernels off the cob; discard the cob. Place the kernels in a large bowl. Add the beans, tomatoes, and onions.

▸ In a small bowl whisk together the mustard, vinegar, and olive oil until well combined. Add the dressing to the vegetables and toss to coat. Add the goat cheese and toss. Season with salt and pepper to taste. Serve warm or chilled.

Serves 4 to 6.

**Cooking Tip:** Blanching is a culinary term for cooking a vegetable until it is just crisp-tender. Bring a medium pot of salted water to a boil. Add the vegetable and cook until vibrant green and crisp-tender, 1 to 1 1/2 minutes. Drain and rinse under cold water to stop the cooking process.

**Do-Ahead:** The vegetables and dressing can be prepped the night before. Toss all the ingredients together before serving.

**Variation:** Feta cheese would be a delicious substitute for the goat cheese in this salad.

# Grilled Avocado BLT Salad

*My friend Emily Nokes Martin always offers a tasty spin on a classic dish. I would have never thought to grill an avocado, but the results add a smoky deliciousness to this salad.*

Vegetable oil, for the grates
2 avocados, halved, seeded, and peeled
4 tablespoons olive oil, divided
Kosher salt and freshly ground black
    pepper
4 cups baby arugula
1 1/2 cups cherry tomatoes, halved

1/4 cup thinly sliced red onions (about 1/2
    small onion)
1/4 cup freshly squeezed lemon juice
1/2 pound bacon (about 10 slices),
    cooked, drained on paper towels, and
    crumbled

▶ Preheat a clean grill to medium with the lid closed for 8 to 10 minutes. Lightly brush the grates with oil.

▶ Lightly brush the avocado halves with 1 tablespoon of the olive oil and season with the salt and pepper to taste.

▶ Place the avocado halves on the grill, cut-side down first. Close the lid and cook until they develop golden brown grill marks, about 2 to 3 minutes per side. Remove from the grill and cut into thin slices.

▶ To serve, place a layer of the arugula on a platter. Add the avocado slices and layer with the cherry tomatoes and the onions. Drizzle the lemon juice and remaining olive oil over the top to taste. Season with salt and pepper to taste. Sprinkle the crumbled bacon evenly over the top. Serve immediately.

Serves 4.

 **Cooking Tip:** For a vegetarian version, just omit the bacon.

# Sandwiches

Gone are the days when dinner was defined as "a meat and two sides."
Easy to fix one-dish items like sandwiches, salads, and quesadillas now
qualify as a proper meal.

*Thank goodness* is my sentiment!

These days I am all about casual, comfortable eating. But easy doesn't
have to translate to boring or bland. The sandwiches hot off my grill are
not your typical brown bag lunch.

When I develop recipes, I look for inspiration in many places. Most
often it comes from a memorable dish at a restaurant or at a friend's table.
I am not shy about asking for a recipe or writing a menu description on
a cocktail napkin! Call me crazy, but I find it fun to go home and see if I
can replicate the same flavors in my kitchen . . . most of the time just from
memory.

The Ultimate Burger (page 168), for example, is from one of my
favorite neighborhood restaurants. The Blackened Snapper Po-Boy (page
177) was inspired by two of my favorite treats from New Orleans (where
I was born, by the way!)—blackened fish and the iconic po-boy sandwich.
The Black Bean Burger (page 161) was one of those items that I tasted at a
friend's house and then begged for the recipe!

The beauty of a good sandwich is that it is mostly assembly—bread,
cheese, and condiments like mustard require no cooking. And no need to
worry about a side dish. The sandwiches in this chapter are so satisfyingly
good, all you will need is a bag of chips.

# Banh Mi with Grilled Pork

*These Vietnamese subs are popping up on menus across the country. Ingredients are mixed and matched at the whim of the kitchen, but there are common denominators to all banh mi—crusty French bread, a bright, crunchy vegetable slaw made with daikon radish and carrots, sliced jalapeño peppers, and fresh cilantro.*

1/2 cup rice vinegar
1 tablespoon sugar
1/2 teaspoon salt
1/2 cup shredded daikon radish
1/2 cup shredded carrots
1 baguette (24-inch), cut into 4 pieces and
    split in half
2 tablespoons unsalted butter, melted
4 tablespoons mayonnaise

1 grilled Honey-Teriyaki Pork Tenderloin
    (page 71), thinly sliced
1/2 cup thinly sliced cucumber
1/2 bunch watercress, woody stems
    removed
2 fresh jalapeños, thinly sliced
1/4 cup chopped fresh cilantro
Sriracha or Asian garlic chili sauce
    (optional)

▶ In a medium bowl whisk together the vinegar, sugar, and salt. Add the shredded radishes and carrots and toss until well coated. Set aside to marinate, stirring occasionally, for 15 minutes. Drain and discard the vinegar mixture.

▶ Lightly brush the insides of the baguette slices with the butter. Toast on a hot grill or under a broiler.

▶ Spread the mayonnaise on the top and bottom of each baguette. Place the sliced pork on the roll. Top with the cucumbers, radish and carrot mixture, watercress, jalapenos, and cilantro. Garnish with the sriracha or Asian garlic chili sauce if desired.

Serves 4.

**Cooking Tip:** Bahn mi sandwiches are a great way to use leftovers. Substitute sliced chicken, steak, or even grilled fish for the pork.

**Variation:** For a vegetarian version, substitute grilled Miso Eggplant (page 197) for the pork.

# Beer Brats with Grilled Peppers and Onions

*Poaching the brats in beer helps add flavor and moisture. With this technique you are guaranteed a nicely grilled sausage with a juicy interior.*

2 (12-ounce) cans beer
4 bratwurst
Vegetable oil, for the grates
1 red bell pepper
1 green bell pepper

1 red onion, cut into 1/4-inch-thick slices
6 tablespoons olive oil, divided
4 hoagie buns, split in half
1/4 cup spicy brown mustard

▶ Place the beer and the bratwurst in a medium saucepan. Over medium-high heat, bring to a simmer and cook until the sausages are just cooked through, about 10 minutes. Drain the sausages.

▶ Preheat a clean grill to medium-high with the lid closed for 8 to 10 minutes. Lightly brush the grates with oil.

▶ Brush the peppers and onion slices with 2 tablespoons of the olive oil. Place the onion slices on the grill and cook until slightly charred and tender, about 2 to 3 minutes per side. Remove from the grill and reserve. Place the whole peppers on the grill and cook until charred on all sides, 8 to 10 minutes total. Transfer the peppers to a bowl, cover, and let rest for 10 minutes before peeling, coring, and thinly slicing.

▶ Lightly brush the sausages with 2 tablespoons of the olive oil and place on the grill. Close the lid and cook, turning frequently, until golden brown on all sides and warmed through, about 10 minutes total.

▶ Brush the inside of the buns with the remaining 2 tablespoons of olive oil. Place on the grill, cut-side down, and cook until lightly toasted, about 1 minute.

▶ Spread the bottom half of each bun with mustard. Top with a sausage and the grilled peppers and onions.

Serves 4.

**Cooking Tips:** If you are worried about your onion slices falling through the grates, you can cook them in a grill basket or place them on skewers.

How can you go wrong when you're cooking with beer?! The better the beer, the better the flavor. Never use what you wouldn't drink.

**Suggested Side:** Smoky Steak Fries (page 191)

# Black Bean Burgers

*Forget the veggie burgers in the frozen food section of your supermarket! Homemade black bean burgers are so much tastier and better for you. Thanks to Nevada Presley for sharing these flavorful vegetarian burgers with me.*

1 can (15-ounce) black beans, drained
  and rinsed
1/4 cup finely diced green bell peppers
  (about 1/2 green bell pepper)
1/4 cup finely diced yellow onions (about
  1/2 small onion)
3 cloves garlic, minced
1 egg

1 tablespoon chili powder
1 1/2 tablespoons cumin
1 teaspoon hot sauce
1/2 cup old-fashioned rolled oats
Vegetable oil, for the grates
4 hamburger buns, split in half
2 ripe avocados, halved, seeded, peeled,
  and sliced

▶ In a medium bowl mash the black beans with a fork until thick and pasty.

▶ Place the bell peppers, onions, and garlic in the food processor and puree. Place the mixture into a fine mesh strainer over another bowl and press to strain the liquid. Add the mixture to the beans and stir to combine. Discard the liquid.

▶ In a small bowl stir together the egg, chili powder, cumin, and hot sauce. Add the egg mixture and the oats to the beans and stir until the mixture is sticky and holds together. Divide into four patties, each about 3/4-inch thick. Cover, place in the refrigerator, and chill for at least an hour or as long as overnight.

▶ Preheat a clean grill to medium-high for 8 to 10 minutes with the lid closed. Lightly brush the grates with oil.

▶ Place the burgers on the grill. Close the lid and cook, turning once, until golden brown and warmed through, 5 to 6 minutes on each side. About 1 minute before the burgers are done, place the buns, cut-side down, on the grill and cook until lightly toasted.

▶ To serve, place each burger on the bottom half of a bun and garnish with avocado slices. Top with the bun tops. Serve immediately.

Serves 4.

 **Cooking Tip:** Do not be tempted to skip the step of draining the pureed vegetables. That extra moisture makes the black bean burgers too sticky to be grilled.

 **Do-Ahead:** The black bean burgers are refrigerated for an hour before cooking to help them keep their shape. The burgers can be assembled as long as 24 hours in advance. Just be sure to cover and refrigerate until ready to grill.

 **Variation:** Nevada adds the egg to help the burgers stay together better. But for a vegan version, just omit the egg and add a tablespoon of veganaise.

# Peppered Steak Sandwiches with Caramelized Onions, Arugula, and Horseradish Mayonnaise

*Make a roast beef sandwich into something extraordinary with peppered filet mignons and caramelized sweet Vidalia onions.*

### For the Horseradish Mayonnaise:
- 1/3 cup mayonnaise
- 2 tablespoons prepared horseradish
- Kosher salt and freshly ground black pepper

### For the Peppered Steak Sandwich:
- Vegetable oil, for the grates
- 2 5- to 6-ounce filet mignons, each about 1 1/4-inches thick
- 3 tablespoons olive oil, divided
- Kosher salt
- 4 tablespoons coarsely ground black pepper
- 1 Vidalia onion, peeled and cut into 1/4-inch slices
- 8 slices French bread
- 1 cup arugula

▶ To make the Horseradish Mayonnaise: In a small bowl whisk together the mayonnaise and horseradish until well combined. Season with the salt and pepper to taste. Cover and refrigerate until ready to serve.

▶ To make the Peppered Steak Sandwiches: Preheat a clean grill to medium-high with the lid closed for 8 to 10 minutes. Lightly brush the grates with oil.

▶ Lightly brush the filets with 2 tablespoons of the olive oil. Season with the salt to taste. Evenly season each filet with the black pepper, pressing down lightly to make the pepper adhere on all sides.

▶ Lightly brush the onion slices with the remaining 1 tablespoon olive oil.

▶ Place the steaks and the onions on the grill. Close the lid. Cook the onions until nicely browned and softened, about 5 to 6 minutes per side. Cook the steaks, turning once, until the desired temperature is reached, 5 to 6 minutes per side for medium-rare or 6 to 7 minutes per side for medium. Remove the steaks from the heat and set aside to rest for 5 minutes before slicing.

▶ Thinly slice each filet.

▶ To serve, place 4 slices of bread on a work surface and evenly spread with the horseradish mayonnaise. Place the sliced beef on the bread and garnish with the grilled onions and the arugula. Top each sandwich half with one of the remaining slices of bread. Serve warm.

Serves 4.

**Cooking Tip:** Sandwiches are a tasty use for leftover steak. This sandwich could also be made with another cut of beef, such as strip steak or flank steak.

# Tuscan Chicken Sandwich

*This is a "backyard" variation on one of the most popular sandwiches I designed for Cheffie's Café. Hope you enjoy it as much as our customers do!*

Vegetable oil, for the grates
1/2 cup mayonnaise
2 tablespoons prepared pesto
4 boneless, skinless chicken breasts
     (about 1 1/2 pounds)
2 tablespoons olive oil
Kosher salt and freshly ground black
     pepper

4 ciabatta rolls
4 thin slices fresh mozzarella
1/2 cup thinly sliced roasted red bell
     peppers
1/4 cup thinly sliced red onions
1 cup fresh baby spinach

▶ Preheat a clean grill to medium-high with the lid closed for 8 to 10 minutes. Lightly brush the grates with oil.

▶ In a small bowl whisk together the mayonnaise and the pesto. Refrigerate until ready to serve.

▶ Lightly brush the chicken breasts with the olive oil and generously season with the salt and pepper.

▶ Place the chicken on the grill. Close the lid and cook, turning once, until no longer pink in the middle, 6 to 8 minutes per side. About 1 minute before the chicken is done, place the rolls, cut-side down, on the grill and cook until lightly toasted.

▶ To serve, spread the pesto mayonnaise on the top and bottom of each roll. Place the chicken on the bread and garnish with mozzarella, peppers, onions, and spinach.

Serves 4.

 **Cooking Tip:** This sandwich is a great way to use leftover grilled chicken.

# Tuna Burgers with Wasabi Slaw

*These burgers have an Asian spin thanks to the addition of fresh ginger and a spicy wasabi slaw.*

**For the Wasabi Slaw:**
- 2 tablespoons wasabi powder
- 1 1/2 tablespoons water
- 1/2 cup mayonnaise
- 1 teaspoon grated fresh ginger
- 1 clove garlic, minced
- 2 cups angel hair coleslaw mix (or finely shredded green cabbage)
- Kosher salt and freshly ground black pepper

**For the Tuna Burgers:**
- 1 pound sushi-grade tuna, cut into 1-inch pieces
- 2 tablespoons Dijon mustard
- 1 clove garlic, minced
- 1 tablespoon finely diced shallots
- 1 tablespoon finely grated fresh ginger
- 1 teaspoon finely grated lemon zest
- Vegetable oil, for the grates
- 4 hamburger buns, split in half

▸ To make the Wasabi Slaw: In a small bowl mix together the wasabi powder and water until a paste is formed. Add the mayonnaise, ginger, and garlic and stir until well combined.

▸ Place the slaw in medium bowl. Add the wasabi mayonnaise and toss until evenly coated. Season with the salt and pepper to taste. Cover and refrigerate until ready to serve.

▸ To make the Tuna Burgers: Place the tuna in a food processor and chop until coarsely ground. Do not over-process. You want the tuna to be minced not pureed, similar to the texture of hamburger meat. Transfer the tuna to a large bowl. Add the mustard, garlic, shallots, ginger, and lemon zest and gently stir to combine. Divide the meat into 4 equal portions. Being careful not to overwork or compact the meat too much, pat each portion into a 3/4-inch-thick patty.

Cover, place in the refrigerator, and chill for at least an hour or as long as overnight.

▸ Preheat a clean grill to medium-high with the lid closed for 8 to 10 minutes. Lightly brush the grates with oil.

▸ Place the burgers on the grill. Close the lid and cook, turning once, until the desired temperature is reached, 3 to 4 minutes per side for medium-rare. About 1 minute before the burgers are done, place the buns, cut-side down, on the grill and cook until lightly toasted.

▸ To serve, place each burger on the bottom half of a bun and garnish with the wasabi slaw. Top each burger with a bun top. Serve immediately.

Serves 4.

**Cooking Tip:** Not a fan of slaw? Then use the wasabi mayonnaise as a condiment rather than a dressing.

**Do-Ahead:** The tuna burgers are refrigerated for an hour before cooking to help them keep their shape. The burgers, as well as the slaw, can be assembled as long as 24 hours in advance. Just be sure to cover and refrigerate until ready to grill.

# The Ultimate Burger

*When I asked chef Jackson Kramer of Interim Restaurant in Memphis, Tennessee, to share his scrumptious burger recipe, he joked "Sure. But it's just a basic burger made with love." Jackson gets his beef from a local farmer who raises his cattle with love and care. This care results in some of the tastiest beef around. So whether you dress up your burger or eat it plain, remember that the key to a juicy, tasty burger is to start with high-quality ground beef.*

### For the Roasted Tomatoes:
4 Roma tomatoes, sliced in half lengthwise
1 tablespoon fresh thyme leaves
2 cloves garlic, minced
2 tablespoons olive oil
Kosher salt and freshly ground black
    pepper

### For the Roasted Garlic Mayonnaise:
1/2 cup mayonnaise
6 cloves roasted garlic

### For the Burger:
Vegetable oil, for the grates
1 1/2 pounds ground chuck or sirloin
Kosher salt and freshly ground black
    pepper
4 slices white cheddar
4 kaiser buns, split in half
1 dill pickle, thinly sliced
4 pieces tender leaf lettuce
8 slices applewood-smoked bacon,
    cooked and drained on paper towels

▶ To make the Roasted Tomatoes: Preheat an oven to 375°F. In a medium mixing bowl, toss the tomatoes with the thyme, garlic, and the oil. Season with the salt and pepper to taste. Place in a single layer, cut-side up, on a baking sheet and cook until the tomatoes are softened, 15 to 20 minutes. Set aside.

▶ To make the Roasted Garlic Mayonnaise: Place the mayonnaise and roasted garlic in a small bowl. Stir to combine. Cover and refrigerate until ready to serve.

▶ To make the Burgers: Preheat a clean grill to medium-high with the lid closed for 8 to 10 minutes. Lightly brush the grates with oil.

▶ Place the ground beef in a large bowl. Generously season with the salt and pepper. Divide the meat into 4 equal portions. Being careful not to overwork or compact the meat too much, pat each portion into a 3/4-inch thick patty.

▶ Place the burgers on the grill. Close the lid and cook until the desired temperature is reached, 4 to 6 minutes per side for medium. About 1 minute before the burgers are done, place a slice of cheese on each burger and allow to melt. Place the buns, cut-side down, on the grill and cook until lightly toasted.

▶ To serve, spread the garlic mayonnaise on the top and bottom of each bun. Place the burgers on the bottom half of the buns and garnish with the roasted tomatoes, pickles, lettuce, and bacon. Top with the bun tops. Serve immediately.

Serves 4.

**Cooking Tips:** When grilling burgers, never flatten them with a spatula—you'll press out all those juices that make burgers so good.

To roast the garlic, preheat your oven to 350°F. Trim about 1/2-inch off the top of a head of garlic, leaving the head intact. Place the garlic in a small baking dish. Drizzle 1 tablespoon of olive oil over the cut top of the garlic. Season with salt and pepper. Cover with aluminum foil and bake until the garlic is soft, about 1 hour.

**Do-Ahead:** The roasted garlic mayonnaise can be made up to 3 days in advance. Store covered in your refrigerator until ready to serve.

# Spinach and Mushroom Quesadilla

*Cooking quesadillas on the grill gives them a deliciously smoky flavor.*

3 tablespoons olive oil, divided
1 pound sliced white button mushrooms
1 garlic clove, minced
1 teaspoon dried thyme leaves
Kosher salt and freshly ground black
    pepper

1 bag (6-ounce) fresh baby spinach
8 fajita-size (6-inch) flour tortillas
1 cup shredded Monterey Jack cheese
Vegetable oil, for the grates

▶ In a large skillet over medium-high heat, warm 2 tablespoons of the olive oil until a few droplets of water sizzle when carefully sprinkled in the pan. Add the mushrooms, garlic, and thyme. Cook, stirring often, until lightly browned, about 5 minutes. Season with the salt and pepper to taste. Remove the mushrooms from the skillet and set aside.

▶ Return the skillet to the stove top and add the remaining 1 tablespoon olive oil. Add the spinach and cook, stirring often, until just wilted, about 1 to 2 minutes.

▶ Place 4 tortillas on a work surface. Evenly sprinkle each with 1/4 cup of the cheese, 1/4 of

the spinach, and 1/4 of the mushrooms. Cover with the remaining tortillas.

▶ Preheat a clean grill to medium-high with the lid closed for 8 to 10 minutes. Lightly brush the grates with oil.

▶ Place the quesadillas on the grill. Close the lid and cook, turning once, until golden brown and the cheese is melted, about 2 to 3 minutes per side.

▶ To serve, cut the quesadillas into wedges and serve warm.

Serves 4.

**Cooking Tip:** The varieties of quesadillas that can be prepared are endless—the only requisite ingredient is cheese. Have fun experimenting with your favorite ingredients.

# Hawaiian Turkey Burgers

*Ground turkey on its own just isn't as flavorful as ground beef. Plumped up with flavorful ingredients like red peppers, mustard, and mango chutney, it becomes a grill-worthy burger.*

1 pound ground turkey (7% fat)
1/4 cup panko bread crumbs
1/4 cup finely diced red bell peppers
1/4 cup thinly sliced scallions (about 2 scallions)
2 tablespoons Dijon mustard
2 tablespoons Major Grey's mango chutney

Kosher salt and freshly ground black pepper
Vegetable oil, for the grates
4 slices fresh pineapple
2 tablespoons canola oil
4 hamburger buns, split in half
1/2 cup teriyaki sauce

▶ In a large mixing bowl combine the ground turkey, bread crumbs, red bell peppers, scallions, Dijon mustard, and chutney. Season with the salt and pepper to taste. Gently stir to combine. Divide the mixture into 4 equal portions. Being careful not to overwork or compact the meat too much, pat each portion into a 3/4-inch-thick patty.

▶ Preheat a clean grill to medium-high with the lid closed for 8 to 10 minutes. Lightly brush the grates with oil.

▶ Place the burgers on the grill. Close the lid and cook, turning once, until cooked through and no longer pink in the middle, 6 to 8 minutes per side. Lightly brush the pineapple slices with the canola oil and grill until golden brown on both sides, 2 to 3 minutes per side. About 1 minute before the burgers are done, place the buns, cut-side down, on the grill and cook until lightly toasted.

▶ To serve, place each burger on the bottom half of the bun and garnish with the teryaki sauce and a slice of pineapple. Top each burger with a bun top. Serve immediately.

Serves 4.

 **Cooking Tip:** Since turkey is so lean, be sure to use ground turkey that is at least 7 percent fat. Using anything leaner will result in dry burgers.

 **Do-Ahead:** Burgers can be formed, tightly wrapped, and refrigerated for up to 24 hours in advance.

# Grilled Salmon Burgers with Dill Tartar Sauce

*Capers and red onions are the signature sides for smoked salmon, so it's no surprise they add a tasty touch to salmon burgers.*

### For the Dill Tartar Sauce:
- 1/2 cup mayonnaise
- 1 tablespoon Dijon mustard
- 1 teaspoon freshly squeezed lemon juice
- 2 tablespoons pickle relish
- 1 tablespoon capers
- 1 tablespoon finely chopped fresh dill
- Kosher salt and freshly ground black pepper

### For the Grilled Salmon Burgers:
- 1 pound salmon, cut into 1-inch pieces
- 1/4 cup panko bread crumbs
- 2 tablespoons Dijon mustard
- 1 clove garlic, minced
- 1 tablespoon finely diced red onions
- 1 tablespoon capers
- Kosher salt and freshly ground black pepper
- Vegetable oil, for the grates
- 4 hamburger buns, split in half

▶ To make the Dill Tartar Sauce: In a small bowl place the mayonnaise, mustard, lemon juice, pickle relish, capers, and dill. Stir until well combined. Season the with salt and pepper to taste. Cover and refrigerate until ready to serve.

▶ To make the Salmon Burgers: Place the salmon in a food processor and chop until coarsely ground. Do not over-process. You want the salmon to be minced not pureed, similar to the texture of hamburger meat. Transfer the salmon to a large bowl. Add the bread crumbs, mustard, garlic, red onions, and capers. Season with the salt and pepper to taste. Gently stir to combine. Divide the mixture into 4 equal portions. Being careful not to overwork or compact the meat too much, pat each portion into a 3/4-inch-thick patty.

▶ Cover, place in the refrigerator, and chill for at least 1 hour or as long as overnight.

▶ Preheat a clean grill to medium-high with the lid closed for 8 to 10 minutes. Lightly brush the grates with oil.

▶ Place the burgers on the grill. Close the lid and cook, turning once, until the desired temperature is reached, 4 to 5 minutes per side for medium. About 1 minute before the burgers are done, place the buns, cut-side down, on the grill and cook until lightly toasted.

▶ To serve, place each burger on the bottom half of a bun and garnish with the Dill Tartar Sauce. Top each burger with a bun top. Serve immediately.

Serves 4.

**Do-Ahead:** The salmon burgers are refrigerated for 1 hour before cooking to help them keep their shape. The burgers, as well as the tartar sauce, can be assembled as long as 24 hours in advance. Just be sure to cover and refrigerate until ready to grill.

# Blackened Snapper Po-Boy

*You can take the girl out of New Orleans, but you can't take the Cajun out of her! This sandwich combines two of my favorite Cajun treats—blackened fish and the po-boy sandwich.*

### For the Remoulade Sauce:
- 3/4 cup mayonnaise
- 4 tablespoons ketchup
- 3 tablespoons freshly squeezed lemon juice
- Kosher salt and freshly ground black pepper
- 1 tablespoon finely sliced scallions

### For the Blackened Snapper:
- Vegetable oil, for the grates
- 4 6-ounce red snapper fillets
- 2 tablespoons olive oil
- 4 tablespoons blackened seasoning
- 4 crusty French rolls, split in half
- 1/2 cup sliced dill pickles
- 4 slices tomatoes
- 4 pieces tender leaf lettuce

▶ To make the Remoulade Sauce: In a medium mixing bowl whisk together the mayonnaise, ketchup, and lemon juice. Season to taste with the salt and pepper. Stir in the scallions. Cover and refrigerate until ready to serve.

▶ To make the Blackened Snapper Po-Boys: Preheat a clean grill to medium-high with the lid closed for 8 to 10 minutes. Lightly brush the grates with oil.

▶ Brush the snapper fillets with the olive oil. Season both sides of the fish with the blackened seasoning.

▶ Place fish on the grill. Close the lid and cook, turning once, until medium, 4 to 5 minutes per side. About 1 minute before the fish is done, place the rolls, cut-side down, on the grill and cook until lightly toasted.

▶ To serve, spread the Remoulade Sauce on the top and bottom of each roll. Place the fish on the bread and garnish with the pickles, tomatoes, and lettuce. Top with the remaining bread and serve immediately.

Serves 4.

**Cooking Tip:** Any firm white fish will work for a grilled fish sandwich.
   Don't like it spicy? Just omit the blackened seasoning and season your fish with salt and pepper.

# Vegetables & Sides

I had more fun developing the recipes for this chapter. I was on a quest to see what could be thrown on a grill and still taste good. Would bok choy (page 213) get that same delicious smokiness as romaine when flame-kissed? What would cherry tomatoes (page 205) and potatoes (page 191) do on a grill? I was thrilled to discover that almost every veggie I tried tasted delicious.

These are all quick and easy sides with lots of flavor. They are simply dressed to let the flavor of the fresh produce take center stage. That's the advantage of using the freshest produce you can find.

I had the benefit (and pleasure) of working on this book with two talented friends who are vegetarians. My dear friend Nevada Presley spent several months working with me on the book as an editor, kitchen assistant, and typist. She had recently received her certification as a natural foods chef and wanted to see firsthand how to write a cookbook. Justin Fox Burks took the absolutely gorgeous photos that you will see throughout *Simply Grilling*. In addition to being an über-talented photographer, he is also a whiz in the kitchen, hosting his own very popular recipe blog *The Chubby Vegetarian*.

As we worked on the book, their love of vegetables started to rub off on me! Their enthusiasm and energy are contagious. Neither is on a soapbox to try to tell you not to eat meat. They keep the reasons for their personal choices to themselves—but they are both eager and happy to share their tasty recipes.

I'll never be a vegetarian—I love a good juicy steak too much—but I am starting to make vegetables, fruit, and other whole ingredients the center of more meals. I am hoping the simple sides in this chapter help you realize, "It's fun to eat your veggies!"

# Cajun Grilled Okra

*Grilled okra is simply delicious! It is yummy as a quick and easy appetizer right off the grill or served as a side.*

Vegetable oil, for the grates
1 pound fresh okra
Skewers (if using bamboo, soak in water
for 30 minutes)

1/4 cup olive oil
1/4 cup Creole seasoning

▸ Preheat a clean grill to medium-high with the lid closed for 8 to 10 minutes. Lightly brush the grates with oil.

▸ Place the okra on skewers. Drizzle with the olive oil until lightly coated. Season to taste with the Creole seasoning.

▸ Grill the okra, turning once, until nicely browned and tender, 2 to 4 minutes per side. Transfer the grilled okra to a platter and serve immediately.

Serves 4.

 **Cooking Tips:** No skewers in the house? No worries. The skewers are used to help make the cooking process simple. Instead, just place the okra pods perpendicular to the grill grates to prevent them from falling through.
    This recipe only works with fresh okra. Frozen okra is not a good substitute.

**Variation:** Feel free to use your favorite seasoning blend. For an extra kick, try a blackened seasoning blend. If you're watching your sodium, try one of the salt-free herb blends. Even just plain old salt and pepper gives delicious results.

# Grilled Asparagus

*Be sure to put your asparagus on the grill perpendicular to the grates. You wouldn't want to lose any of these yummy veggies!*

Vegetable oil, for the grates
1 bunch (about 1 pound) asparagus,
 tough woody ends snapped off and
 discarded

2 tablespoons olive oil
Kosher salt and freshly ground black
 pepper

▶ Preheat a clean grill to medium-high with the lid closed for 8 to 10 minutes. Lightly brush the grates with oil.

▶ Place the asparagus on a baking sheet. Toss with the olive oil until well coated. Season with the salt and pepper to taste.

▶ Place the asparagus on the grill. Cook, turning once or twice, until tender and slightly charred, 3 to 5 minutes on each side. Serve immediately.

Serves 4.

**Cooking Tip:** The ends of asparagus spears tend to be tough and woody. To trim, simply bend each stalk, and it will naturally break off in just the right spot.

**Variations:** Grilled asparagus makes a perfect side dish, but it also makes a tasty salad. See page 133 for my Asparagus and Cherry Tomato Salad.

# Grilled Lime Sweet Potatoes

*I am a big fan of sweet potatoes, and this is one of my favorite ways to enjoy them. The lime makes them the perfect accompaniment for a Mexican- or Caribbean-inspired meal.*

Vegetable oil, for the grill screen
2 medium sweet potatoes (about 1 1/2
    pounds), peeled and sliced into
    rounds about 1/4-inch thick
2 tablespoons olive oil

Kosher salt and freshly ground black
    pepper
1 tablespoon lime zest
2 tablespoons freshly squeezed lime juice

▶ Preheat a clean grill with a grill screen to medium with the lid closed for 8 to 10 minutes. Lightly brush the grill screen with oil.

▶ Place the sweet potatoes and the olive oil in a large bowl. Toss until well coated. Season with the salt and pepper to taste.

▶ Place the potatoes on the grill screen. Close the lid and cook, turning once, until tender and golden brown, 7 to 8 minutes total. Place in a serving bowl and toss with the lime zest and juice. Serve warm.

Serves 4.

 **Cooking Tips:** If you don't have a grill screen, you can line the grill with aluminum foil to prevent the potatoes from falling through the grates.

 **Variation:** Lime doesn't go with your main course? Then just omit it, and you'll have simply delicious grilled sweet potatoes.

# Grilled Summer Squash

*Grilling baskets help small-cut vegetables like these from falling through the grates. If you don't own one, you can place a piece of aluminum foil on the grill.*

Vegetable oil, for the grill basket or screen
1 zucchini, cut into 1/2-inch slices
1 yellow squash, cut into 1/2-inch slices
1 yellow onion, thinly sliced
1/4 cup olive oil

1 tablespoon dried Italian seasoning
Kosher salt and freshly ground black
    pepper
Parmesan shavings, for garnish

▶ Preheat a clean grill with a grill basket or screen to medium-high with the lid closed for 8 to 10 minutes. Lightly brush the basket or screen with oil.

▶ In a large bowl toss together the zucchini, yellow squash, onions, olive oil, and Italian seasoning. Season with the salt and pepper to taste.

▶ Place the vegetables in the grill basket. Close the lid and cook, turning once or twice, until the vegetables are tender, about 5 minutes per side.

▶ To serve, garnish with Parmesan shavings.

Serves 4.

**Cooking Tip:** I love the presentation shaved Parmesan makes. To shave this or any hard cheese, use a vegetable peeler to slice it into paper-thin slivers.

# Lemony Grilled Fennel

*Fennel is an interesting vegetable. Raw, it has a strong licorice flavor, but when cooked, it has a milder and sweeter flavor. Grilled with a hint of lemon, fennel makes the perfect vegetable side dish to any grilled meat or seafood dish.*

Vegetable oil, for the grates
2 fennel bulbs
3 tablespoons olive oil, divided
Kosher salt and freshly ground black
      pepper

1/4 cup freshly squeezed lemon juice
2 tablespoons freshly grated lemon zest

▶ Preheat a clean grill to medium with the lid closed for 8 to 10 minutes. Lightly brush the grates with oil.

▶ Trim the top and the bottom of the root from each fennel bulb and discard them. Cut each bulb into quarters.

▶ Brush the fennel with 2 tablespoons of the olive oil. Season with the salt and pepper to taste.

▶ Place the fennel on the grill, cut-side down. Close the lid and cook, turning once or twice, until tender, about 3 to 4 minutes per side.

▶ Place the fennel on a platter and drizzle with the remaining olive oil, lemon juice, and lemon zest. Serve warm.

Serves 4.

**Cooking Tips:** When purchasing fennel, look for larger round bulbs as they are usually more tender than long slender bulbs. Crisp stalks with bright, feathery fronds are a sign of freshness.
    Don't throw away the feathery fronds left over after trimming your fennel. Similar in texture to fresh dill, the fronds make a delicious addition to a salad.

# Smoky Steak Fries

*These smoky fries are a favorite in my kitchen because they are made without the extra fat and mess of frying. Most often, I season mine with fresh herbs, but for an extra kick I sometimes use a spicy seasoning blend or dry rub.*

4 potatoes, Yukon Gold or Russet,
    scrubbed and cut lengthwise into 6 to
    8 spears
Kosher salt
Vegetable oil, for the grates

1/4 cup olive oil
2 tablespoons fresh thyme leaves, or
    2 teaspoons dried thyme leaves
Kosher salt and freshly ground black
    pepper

▶ Put the potato spears in a large pot and cover with cold salted water. Bring to a boil over high heat and then lower the temperature to a simmer. Cook just until they are tender but still firm, about 8 minutes. Drain and pat dry.

▶ Preheat a clean grill to medium-high with the lid closed for 8 to 10 minutes. Lightly brush the grates with oil.

▶ Brush the potatoes with the olive oil, sprinkle with the thyme, and season with the salt and pepper to taste.

▶ Place the potato spears on the grill. Close the lid and cook, turning the potatoes occasionally, until browned on all sides and cooked through, about 15 minutes total. Serve hot.

Serves 4 to 6.

 **Cooking Tips:** Be sure to reduce the temperature of the water right when it comes to a boil. You want to cook the potatoes at a gentle simmer so they do not break.

    Boiling the potatoes before grilling ensures that you will have fries with a nice crispy crust and a soft-done interior.

# Spinach-Stuffed Portobello Mushrooms

*These meaty portobello mushrooms make a satisfying meal when paired with a simple salad.*

Vegetable oil, for the grates
4 large portobello mushrooms
4 tablespoons olive oil, divided
2 6-ounce bags fresh baby spinach
2 cloves garlic, minced
1/2 teaspoon freshly grated nutmeg

1/4 cup finely diced red bell peppers (half a
  small pepper)
1/4 cup chopped pecans
1/2 cup crumbled feta cheese
Kosher salt and freshly ground black
  pepper

▶ Preheat a clean grill to medium with the lid closed for 8 to 10 minutes. Lightly brush the grates with oil.

▶ Remove the stems from the mushrooms and discard. Use a spoon to scrape the gills from the caps and discard. Set the mushrooms aside.

▶ In a large pan over medium heat, warm 2 tablespoons of the olive oil until a few droplets of water sizzle when carefully sprinkled in the pan. Add the spinach, garlic, and nutmeg. Sauté, stirring occasionally, until the spinach is wilted, 3 to 4 minutes. Remove from the heat and add the red bell peppers, pecans, and feta cheese. Stir to combine. Season with the salt and pepper to taste.

▶ Brush the mushroom caps on both sides with the remaining 2 tablespoons olive oil and season with salt and pepper to taste. Place on a baking sheet or platter, stem side up. Spoon the spinach mixture over the mushroom caps.

▶ Place the mushrooms, spinach side up, directly onto the grill. Close the lid and cook until the mushrooms are tender and cooked through, about 15 to 18 minutes. Serve warm.

Serves 4.

**Cooking Tip:** The sautéed spinach is the basis for the stuffed mushroom. Feel free to substitute your favorite cheeses (Parmesan, goat, or white cheddar for example) or add cooked Italian sausage for a heartier rendition.

**Variation:** For a simple spinach stuffed portobello, omit the red bell peppers and pecans.

# Pete's Baked Beans

*My friend Pete Niedbala came up with the brilliant idea of using several types of beans in this classic picnic side. The variety of beans adds both flavor and color to this simple dish.*

1 can (15-ounce) black eyed peas, drained
1 can (15-ounce) black beans, drained
1 can (15-ounce) red kidney beans, drained
1 can (15-ounce) pinto beans, drained
1 bottle (12-ounce) chili sauce
4 tablespoons prepared yellow mustard
1 1/2 cups light brown sugar

1/2 pound bacon (about 10 slices), cooked, drained on paper towels, and crumbled
1/2 cup finely diced yellow onions (one small onion)
Kosher salt and freshly ground black pepper
Hot sauce, to taste

▸ Preheat a clean grill to medium-high with the lid closed for 8 to 10 minutes.

▸ Place the black eyed peas, black beans, red kidney beans, pinto beans, chili sauce, yellow mustard, brown sugar, bacon, and onions in a cast-iron Dutch oven. Stir until well combined. Season with the salt and pepper to taste.

▸ Place the pan directly on the grates and close the lid. Cook, stirring occasionally, until the flavors have melded and the beans have slightly softened, about 30 to 35 minutes. Season with hot sauce if desired.

Serves 6 to 8.

**Cooking Tip:** I usually have this dish cooking off to one side of my grill while I am cooking the entrée on the other side.

**Variation:** For a vegetarian version, omit the bacon.

# Miso Eggplant

*Most people think of miso as a type of soup, but this traditional Japanese seasoning makes a delicious marinade for vegetables.*

2 tablespoons white (shiro) miso paste
2 tablespoons water
2 tablespoons soy sauce
1 tablespoon olive oil
2 medium eggplant, cut crosswise into
    1/2-inch-thick slices

Vegetable oil, for the grates
Kosher salt and freshly ground black
    pepper

▸ In a shallow nonreactive dish just large enough to hold the eggplant slices in a single layer, stir together the white miso paste, water, soy sauce, and olive oil. Place the eggplant in the marinade and gently toss until well coated. Cover, place in the refrigerator, and marinate for 30 minutes.

▸ Preheat a clean grill to medium-high with the lid closed for 8 to 10 minutes. Lightly brush the grates with oil.

▸ Remove the eggplant from the marinade and shake off the excess. Discard the marinade. Season with the salt and pepper to taste.

▸ Place the eggplant slices on the grill. Close the lid and cook, turning once, until tender, 3 to 4 minutes per side. Serve warm or chilled.

Serves 4 to 6.

**Cooking Tip:** Miso paste is a traditional Japanese seasoning made from fermented soybeans. There are two main varieties available: red (aka) or white (shiro). Look for it in the Asian foods or refrigerator sections of your local market.

**Marinate:** 30 minutes.

# Mexican Corn on the Cob

*Every time I go to Las Tortugas, an authentic Mexican deli in Germantown, Tennessee, I order their "Elote." This sweet yet fiery corn on the cob is a popular street food in Mexico. Luckily for us, this deliciously different dish is easy to make at home.*

Vegetable oil, for the grates
4 ears fresh corn, shucked
2 tablespoons unsalted butter, room
   temperature

1 cup cotija cheese, crumbled
4 tablespoons mayonnaise
Cayenne pepper
4 lime wedges

▶ Preheat a clean grill to medium-high with the lid closed for 8 to 10 minutes. Lightly brush the grates with oil.

▶ Brush the corn with the butter. Grill the corn, turning occasionally, until just tender and slightly charred on all sides, 8 to 10 minutes total. Remove from the grill.

▶ Spread the cheese on a large plate. While the corn is still warm, spread 1 tablespoon of mayonnaise evenly over each cob. Roll the cob in the cheese, sprinkle with the cayenne pepper to taste, and finish with a squeeze of lime.

Serves 4.

 **Cooking Tip:** Cotija cheese is a salty, semi-hard, crumbly cheese that resembles grated Parmesan. Grated Parmesan or crumbled feta are acceptable substitutes.

**Variation:** Want a simple grilled corn? Minus the toppings, this is the basic technique for grilling corn on the cob.

# Japanese Eggplant with Fresh Tomatoes, Basil, and Goat Cheese

*Every summer I grow tender Japanese eggplant in my garden. This is my favorite way to enjoy this straight-from-the-garden treat.*

Vegetable oil, for the grates
4 Japanese eggplant, stems removed and
     cut in half lengthwise
4 tablespoons olive oil
Kosher salt and freshly ground black
     pepper

1 cup diced tomatoes
1/4 cup chopped fresh basil
2/3 cup crumbled goat cheese
1/2 cup balsamic vinegar

▸ Preheat a clean grill to medium-high with the lid closed for 8 to 10 minutes. Lightly brush the grates with oil.

▸ Brush the eggplant evenly with the olive oil and season with the salt and pepper to taste.

▸ Place the eggplant on the grill, cut-side down. Close the lid and cook, turning once, until tender, about 3 minutes per side.

▸ Place the eggplant on a platter. Top with the tomatoes, basil, and goat cheese. Drizzle the vinegar over the top to taste. Serve immediately.

Serves 4.

**Cooking Tip:** Japanese eggplant, also known as baby eggplant, are longer and skinnier than globe eggplant. They also tend to be more tender and less bitter. If you can't find Japanese eggplant, you can substitute any varietal.

# Grilled Zucchini Ribbons with Fresh Mint and Pine Nuts

*This a great dish to have in your repertoire. It's simple to prepare, makes a statement, and can be served warm or chilled.*

Vegetable oil, for the grates
3 medium zucchini
1/4 cup olive oil, divided
Kosher salt and freshly ground black
    pepper
1/4 teaspoon crushed red pepper flakes
1 clove garlic, minced

2 tablespoons freshly squeezed lemon
    juice
1 tablespoon red wine vinegar
2 tablespoons chopped fresh mint leaves
3 tablespoons toasted pine nuts
Shaved Parmesan (optional garnish)

▶ Preheat a clean grill to medium-high with the lid closed for 8 to 10 minutes. Lightly brush the grates with oil.

▶ Trim the ends of the zucchini and thinly slice lengthwise. Arrange the slices on a baking sheet and drizzle with 2 tablespoons of the olive oil, turning the slices to coat both sides with the oil. Season with the salt, pepper, and red pepper flakes to taste.

▶ Place the zucchini on the grill and cook, turning once, until just tender, 1 to 3 minutes per side. Do not overcook. Place the zucchini slices on a baking sheet, overlapping as little as possible, to cool slightly.

▶ Place the cooled zucchini in a large bowl. Add the garlic, lemon juice, vinegar, remaining 2 tablespoons of olive oil, mint, and pine nuts. Gently toss to combine. Season with salt and pepper to taste. Garnish with shaved Parmesan if desired.

Serves 4.

 **Cooking Tip:** Ideally the zucchini should be sliced about 1/4-inch thick. Use a mandolin or vegetable peeler to help you thinly slice the zucchini.

 **Variation:** Serve this side on top of grilled bread for a delicious appetizer.

# Grilled Cherry Tomatoes with Sweet Basil Vinaigrette

*There is nothing better in the summer than fresh tomatoes. Did you know they are also delicious grilled? You can use all red tomatoes, but for a dramatic presentation I prefer to use a combination of colorful heirloom varietals.*

Vegetable oil, for the grates
16 large cherry tomatoes
Skewers (if using bamboo, soak in water for 30 minutes)
4 tablespoons olive oil, divided

Kosher salt and freshly ground black pepper
2 tablespoons red wine vinegar
3 tablespoons chopped fresh basil

▶ Preheat a clean grill to medium-high with the lid closed for 8 to 10 minutes. Lightly brush the grates with oil.

▶ Thread the tomatoes on the skewers. Brush the tomatoes with 2 tablespoons of the olive oil. Season with the salt and pepper to taste.

▶ Place the tomatoes on the grill. Close the lid and cook the tomatoes until soft and charred, about 4 minutes per side. Transfer the tomatoes to a serving platter.

▶ In a small bowl whisk together the remaining 2 tablespoons olive oil, the red wine vinegar, and the basil. Drizzle the vinaigrette over the grilled tomatoes. Serve warm.

Serves 4.

**Cooking Tip:** I like to thread the tomatoes onto two skewers to prevent them from rolling around.

**Variation:** This recipe works well with whole tomatoes. Cut them in half horizontally and grill about 8 minutes per side.

# Grilled Lime Scallions

*These scallions are a great addition to almost any grilled dish. Serve them on burgers or as a side for a grilled steak or chicken breast. My friend Ashley Woodman deserves all the credit for the secret ingredient in this recipe—a squeeze of lime!*

Vegetable oil, for the grates
1 bunch scallions (about 12), trimmed

1 tablespoon olive oil
2 tablespoons freshly squeezed lime juice

▸ Preheat a clean grill to medium with the lid closed for 8 to 10 minutes. Lightly brush the grates with oil.

▸ Lightly brush the scallions with the olive oil.

▸ Place the scallions on the grill. Close the lid and cook, turning once or twice, until tender, 3 to 4 minutes total.

▸ Place the scallions on a platter and drizzle with the lime juice.

Serves 4.

**Cooking Tip:** Scallions are also known as spring onions or green onions. To trim, remove and discard the root ends.

# Grilled Radicchio with Balsamic Vinegar and Feta

*Do you ever eat something at a restaurant that is so good you are inspired to try to make it at home? My friend Lacy Apperson came up with this recipe after eating at one of her favorite neighborhood dining spots. Thanks Bari Ristorante for providing the inspiration for this delicious side dish.*

Vegetable oil, for the grates
2 heads radicchio, cut into quarters
2 tablespoons olive oil
Kosher salt and freshly ground black
    pepper

1/4 cup balsamic vinegar
1/2 cup crumbled feta

▸ Preheat a clean grill to medium-high with the lid closed for 8 to 10 minutes. Lightly brush the grates with oil.

▸ Brush the radicchio with the olive oil. Season with the salt and pepper to taste.

▸ Place the radicchio on the grill, cut-side down. Close the lid and cook, turning once, until caramelized and fork-tender, 3 to 4 minutes per side.

▸ Place the radicchio on a platter and drizzle with balsamic vinegar to taste. Sprinkle the feta over the top just before serving.

Serves 4.

 **Cooking Tip:** When cutting the radicchio into quarters, be sure to leave a bit of the core intact so it holds together.

 **Variation:** This dish would also be good with crumbled blue cheese.

# Grilled Polenta Cakes with White Wine Mushrooms

*Grilled polenta makes a delicious base for such toppings as sautéed mushrooms, melted blue cheese, and roasted tomatoes.*

### For the Grilled Polenta Cakes:

3 cups water
1 cup polenta
2 tablespoons grated Parmesan, plus extra
    for optional garnish
1 tablespoon unsalted butter, plus extra to
    grease the casserole dish
Kosher salt and freshly ground black pepper
Vegetable oil, for the grates

### For the White Wine Mushrooms:

2 tablespoons olive oil
1 pound sliced baby portobello
    mushrooms
1 clove garlic, minced
1 teaspoon dried thyme leaves
3 tablespoons white wine
2 tablespoons chopped flat-leaf parsley
Kosher salt and freshly ground black pepper

▶ To make the Grilled Polenta Cakes: Bring the water to a boil in a large, heavy pot over high heat. Gradually whisk in the polenta. Reduce the heat to low and cook, stirring often, until the mixture thickens and the polenta is tender, 15 to 20 minutes. Remove the pot from the heat. Add the cheese and butter and stir until melted. Season with the salt and pepper to taste.

▶ Lightly grease a 9- x 9-inch casserole dish with butter. Spoon the polenta into the casserole dish and spread evenly. Refrigerate for at least 2 hours, or until set.

▶ To make the White Wine Mushrooms: In a large skillet over medium-high heat, warm the olive oil until a few droplets of water sizzle when carefully sprinkled in the pan. Add the mushrooms, garlic, and thyme. Cook, stirring often, until lightly browned, about 5 minutes. Add the white wine and cook until the wine has evaporated, about 3 more minutes. Stir in the parsley. Season with the salt and pepper to taste. Remove from the heat and cover to keep warm.

▶ To finish the dish: Preheat a clean grill to medium-high with the lid closed for 8 to 10 minutes. Lightly brush the grates with oil.

Cut the chilled polenta into triangles or squares. Place the polenta on the grill. Cook, turning once, until crisp with golden grill marks, about 4 minutes per side.

To serve, top with the cooked mushrooms. Garnish with freshly grated Parmesan cheese if desired.

Serves 6.

**Cooking Tip:** For grilling, polenta needs to be thick rather than creamy. Don't be tempted to add more liquid, or you will have a melted mess on your grill!

**Do-Ahead:** The longer the polenta chills before grilling, the better. I usually make my polenta the night before and store it covered in the refrigerator until ready to grill.

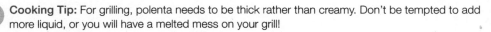

# Grilled Bok Choy with Ponzu Ginger Sauce

*I prefer to use baby bok choy because it is more tender than the regular size. That said, you can use the larger heads of bok choy for this recipe if you prefer.*

### For the Ponzu Ginger Sauce:
- 1/4 cup soy sauce
- 2 tablespoons water
- 1 tablespoon rice vinegar
- 1 tablespoon freshly squeezed lime juice
- 1/2 tablespoon grated fresh peeled ginger
- 1 scallion, thinly sliced

### For the Grilled Bok Choy:
- Vegetable oil, for the grates
- 4 heads baby bok choy (about 1 pound total)
- 2 tablespoons toasted sesame oil
- Kosher salt and freshly ground black pepper

▸ To make the Ponzu Ginger Sauce: In a small bowl whisk together the soy sauce, water, vinegar, lime juice, ginger, and scallion. Cover and refrigerate until ready to serve.

▸ To make the Bok Choy: Preheat a clean grill to medium with the lid closed for 8 to 10 minutes. Lightly brush the grates with oil.

▸ Cut the bok choy heads in half lengthwise. Lightly brush the bok choy with the sesame oil. Season with the salt and pepper to taste.

▸ Place the bok choy on the grill, cut-side down. Close the lid and cook, turning once or twice, until tender and lightly charred, 3 to 4 minutes per side.

▸ Place the bok choy on a platter and drizzle with ponzu ginger sauce to taste. Serve immediately.

Serves 4.

 **Cooking Tip:** I find that the toasted sesame oil adds a nice flavor to this Asian-inspired dish. For a more neutral-flavored bok choy, substitute olive or vegetable oil.

**Do-Ahead:** The Ponzu Ginger Sauce can be made the night before. Cover and refrigerate until ready to use.

# Sweet Endings

In my humble opinion, a meal is not complete without dessert. So, of course, I had to share some of my favorite "sweet endings" with you.

Grilling fruit may seem like a crazy idea to some, but it actually makes sense when you think about it. Fruit is full of natural sugars that caramelize when grilled. A quick sauce or a scoop of ice cream and you're done.

There are a few simple rules to grilling fruit. Make sure that you choose fruits that will hold their shape and texture when grilled. Pineapples, bananas, and stone fruits like peaches, plums, and apricots work best. Also, you will need to add a touch of oil to keep the fruit from sticking. I suggest using a neutral-tasting oil like canola oil so the flavor of the fruit takes center stage. Butter can also be used since it will complement the fruit. Never use olive oil. And don't forget, you always need to start with a clean grill. You don't want your dessert to taste like last night's burgers!

A good friend gave me a challenge for this book—create a chocolate dessert for the grill. It took some creativity, but I think you'll find that my Chocolate-Hazelnut and Banana Panini (page 219) will satisfy the sweet tooth of every chocoholic at your table!

I also couldn't help but include a few of my summertime favorites that aren't off the grill. Desserts like Strawberry Cake (page 235), Luscious Lemon Tart (page 225), and Grasshopper Ice-Box Cake (page 221) are requested over and over again by my family.

# Café au Lait Granita

*This is the ultimate iced coffee treat!*

2/3 cup granulated sugar
4 cups hot brewed double-strength coffee
    or espresso
2 cups heavy cream, divided

1 tablespoon pure vanilla extract
2 tablespoons confectioners' sugar

▶ In a medium bowl stir the granulated sugar into the hot coffee or espresso until dissolved. Add 1 cup of the heavy cream and vanilla and stir to combine. Refrigerate until chilled.

▶ Pour the cooled coffee mixture into a shallow baking dish and freeze until ice crystals begin to form around the edges, about 1 hour. Using a fork, stir and scrape around the edges to break up the ice. Return to the freezer and stir and scrape with a fork every 30 minutes until the mixture is frozen and has a feathery, flaky texture, 2 to 3 hours.

▶ In a medium bowl whip the remaining 1 cup heavy cream with the confectioner' sugar until stiff.

▶ To serve, spoon the granita into individual bowls and top with the whipped cream.

Serves 6.

**Cooking Tip:** Your freezing time will vary, depending on the temperature and strength of your freezer.

**V** **Variation:** Don't like dairy? Just omit the heavy cream from this recipe for an espresso granita treat.

# Chocolate-Hazelnut and Banana Panini

*Elvis had his peanut butter and banana sandwich, but this Memphian prefers this chocolaty version!*

Vegetable oil, for the grates
8 tablespoons unsalted butter (1 stick), at
    room temperature
8 slices white or wheat bread

2/3 cup chocolate-hazelnut spread
2 ripe bananas, sliced

▸ Preheat a clean grill to medium-high with the lid closed for 8 to 10 minutes. Lightly brush the grates with oil.

▸ Evenly butter one side of each slice of bread. Place 4 slices, buttered side down, on a work surface. On each slice, evenly spread the chocolate-hazelnut spread. Add the banana slices. Top each sandwich half with one of the remaining buttered slices of bread, buttered side up.

▸ Place the sandwiches on the grill. Close the lid and cook, turning once, until golden brown, 2 to 3 minutes per side. Remove from the grill. Serve immediately.

Serves 4.

**V** **Variation:** Take Elvis's lead and substitute peanut butter for the chocolate-hazelnut spread.

# Grasshopper Icebox Cake

*Make a show stopping cake without turning on your oven! This cool and creamy no-bake cake is sure to be a hit at your next barbecue.*

Nonstick cooking spray
2 quarts mint chocolate chip ice cream, softened
1 box (9-ounce) chocolate wafer cookies

1 cup chocolate sauce
1 cup crushed cream-filled chocolate sandwich cookies

▶ Spray a 9-inch loaf pan with nonstick cooking spray and line with plastic wrap, allowing a 2-inch overhang on all sides.

▶ Evenly spread half of the ice cream in the bottom of the prepared pan. Place a double layer of chocolate wafer cookies on top of the ice cream. Spread the remaining ice cream evenly over the cookies. Place another layer of cookies over the top. Cover with the plastic overhang. Freeze until firm, at least 4 hours or overnight.

▶ To unmold, let the cake stand at room temperature for 5 minutes. Invert onto a serving plate and remove the pan and the plastic wrap. Garnish the top with chocolate sauce and crushed chocolate sandwich cookies. Slice and serve immediately.

Serves 8.

**Cooking Tip:** Chocolate wafer cookies are available in either the cookie or baking department of your local supermarket. Crushed chocolate sandwich cookies can be substituted if your store doesn't carry them.

**Do-Ahead:** This cake can be made up to 4 days in advance. Keep frozen and tightly wrapped in plastic wrap until ready to serve.

**Variation:** Feel free to substitute your favorite flavors of ice cream.

# Grilled Bananas Foster

*Grilling the bananas adds a delicious touch to this famous New Orleans dessert. I like to grill my bananas in their skins to keep them from falling apart on the grill.*

Vegetable oil, for the grates
1/2 cup (1 stick) plus 2 tablespoons
    unsalted butter, divided
4 firm but ripe bananas

1/2 cup light brown sugar
1/4 cup dark rum
1 pint vanilla ice cream

▶ Preheat a clean grill to medium-high with the lid closed for 8 to 10 minutes. Lightly brush the grates with oil.

▶ Melt 2 tablespoons of the butter in the microwave on low power for 20 to 25 seconds. Leaving the skin on, cut the bananas in half lengthwise. Brush the bananas with the butter and place them on the grill, cut-side down. Close the grill and cook until lightly golden brown, 2 to 3 minutes. Turn the bananas over and continue cooking until the skin begins to pull away from the banana, 1 to 2 more minutes. Transfer to a plate and remove and discard the skins.

▶ In a large saucepan over medium heat, melt the remaining 1/2 cup butter. Add the brown sugar and cook until the sugar dissolves, stirring constantly. Add the rum and stir. If using a gas stove, gently tip the pan to cause the rum to flame. If using an electric stove, ignite the sauce with a BBQ lighter or long match. Continue cooking until the flame dies out, 2 to 3 minutes. Add the grilled bananas and cook until just warmed through, 2 to 3 more minutes.

▶ To serve, place the bananas and a generous spoonful of the sauce in a bowl. Top with the vanilla ice cream and serve immediately.

Serves 4.

**Cooking Tip:** Firm, just-ripe bananas will hold their shape better on the grill than ripe bananas.

# Luscious Lemon Tart

*A lemon tart with a graham cracker pecan crust is surprisingly simple and makes an elegant ending to a meal. I like to serve mine with whipped cream and fresh berries.*

### For the Crust:
- 2/3 cup pecans, lightly toasted and cooled
- 1 cup graham cracker crumbs
- 1/4 cup sugar
- 4 tablespoons (1/2 stick) unsalted butter, melted and cooled to room temperature

### For the Filling:
- 2 large egg yolks
- 1 can (14-ounce) sweetened condensed milk
- 1/2 cup freshly squeezed lemon juice

▶ Preheat the oven to 350°F.

▶ To make the Crust: In a food processor, finely grind the pecans, graham cracker crumbs, and sugar. Add the butter and pulse until well incorporated and moist lumps form.

▶ Transfer to a 9-inch tart pan with a removable bottom. Press the crust evenly into the bottom and up the side. Bake until set, about 8 minutes. Cool on a wire rack.

▶ To make the Filling: In a large bowl beat the egg yolks with the condensed milk. Whisk in the lemon juice, a little at a time, until the filling is well combined. Spoon the filling into the crust.

▶ Bake until the filling is set, about 15 minutes. Let the pie cool to room temperature on a wire rack. Chill for at least one hour before serving.

Serves 8.

**Cooking Tip:** Have a nut allergy? Substitute an additional 2/3 cup of graham cracker crumbs for the pecans.

# Mixed Berry Crumble

*A closed grill works just like an oven, making it perfect for simple desserts such as this berry crumble.*

## For the Filling:

2 cups fresh blueberries
2 cups fresh raspberries
2 cups fresh blackberries
1/2 cup sugar
2 tablespoons all-purpose flour
1/2 teaspoon ground cinnamon
1/4 teaspoon salt

## For the Topping:

1/2 cup all-purpose flour
1/4 cup old-fashioned rolled oats (not instant)
1/4 teaspoon baking powder
1/4 teaspoon Kosher salt
3 tablespoons unsalted butter, room temperature
1/4 cup sugar
Vanilla ice cream (optional)

▶ Preheat a clean grill to medium-high with the lid closed for 8 to 10 minutes.

▶ To make the Filling: In a large bowl combine the blueberries, raspberries, blackberries, sugar, flour, cinnamon, and salt. Place the fruit mixture in a 2-quart disposable foil pan. Cover the pan tightly with foil.

▶ Place the foil pan on the rack in the center of grill. Close the lid and cook for 30 minutes.

▶ To make the Topping: In a medium mixing bowl, stir together the flour, oats, baking powder, and salt. In the bowl of an electric mixer fitted with the paddle attachment, beat the butter and sugar until light and fluffy. Add the dry ingredients and mix until just combined and the mixture has a crumbly texture. (Be careful not to overmix.)

▶ To finish the dish: Uncover the pan and sprinkle the topping evenly over the fruit mixture. Close the lid and cook until the mixture is bubbly and the topping is golden brown, 10 to 15 minutes more.

▶ Cool on a wire rack for 10 minutes. Serve warm, with a scoop of vanilla ice cream, if desired.

Serves 8.

**V** **Variation:** This same technique could be used to make a peach or apple crumble. Just thinly slice the fruit.

# Grilled Pineapple with Rum Caramel Sauce

*Two of my favorite Caribbean flavors—pineapple and rum—come together to make a scrumptious backyard barbecue finale.*

### For the Rum Caramel Sauce:
1 cup sugar
1/4 cup water
3/4 cup heavy cream
2 tablespoons unsalted butter, cut into
   1/2-inch cubes
2 tablespoons dark rum

### For the Grilled Pineapple:
Vegetable oil, for the grates
1 pineapple, peeled, cored, and sliced into
   1/2-inch-thick slices
2 tablespoons canola oil
1 pint vanilla ice cream

▶ To make the Rum Caramel Sauce: In a medium sauce pan with tall sides, place the sugar and water and whisk to combine. Place over medium-high heat and cook until the sugar dissolves, 2 to 3 minutes. Raise the heat to high and continue to cook, without stirring, until the sugar is an amber color. Remove from the heat and carefully stir in 1/4 cup of the heavy cream. (Be careful because the mixture will bubble and sputter as the cream is added.) Gradually stir in the rest of the cream until it is all incorporated. Add the butter and stir until melted. Stir in the rum. Keep warm until ready to serve.

▶ To make the Grilled Pineapple: Preheat a clean grill to medium-high with the lid closed for 8 to 10 minutes. Lightly brush the grates with oil.

▶ Brush both sides of each pineapple slice with the canola oil.

▶ Place the pineapple slices on the grill and cook until lightly golden brown on both sides, 2 to 3 minutes per side.

▶ To serve, place the warm pineapple slices in a bowl. Add a generous spoonful of the sauce and top with vanilla ice cream. Serve immediately.

Serves 4.

**Cooking Tip:** For a nonalcoholic version of the caramel sauce, just omit the rum.

**Do-Ahead:** The caramel sauce can be made up to 2 weeks ahead. Refrigerate until ready to serve.

# Grilled Peaches and Pound Cake

*Nothing says summer more than peaches and grilling, so why not enjoy them together? Grill the pound cake until it's crisp and toasty, then top it with warm, tender grilled peaches and vanilla ice cream. Simply divine!*

Vegetable oil, for the grates
4 ripe peaches, halved and pitted
1 pound cake loaf (homemade or store-bought), sliced 3/4-inch thick

6 tablespoons unsalted butter, melted
1 pint vanilla ice cream
4 tablespoons honey

▶ Preheat a clean grill to medium with the lid closed for 8 to 10 minutes. Lightly brush the grates with oil.

▶ Brush the cut sides of each peach half and both sides of the pound cake slices with the melted butter.

▶ Place the peaches on the grill, cut-side down. Close the lid and cook until grill marks appear, about 3 minutes. Turn and cook until the peach softens and is just heated through, 4 minutes more. Remove the peaches from the grill.

▶ Grill the pound cake slices until lightly toasted, about 2 minutes on each side. Place 2 cake slices on each plate, spoon on the grilled peaches, top with the ice cream, and drizzle with the honey. Serve warm.

Serves 4.

**Cooking Tip:** When buying peaches, look for fruit with a fragrant aroma and flesh that yields a bit when pressed gently. If a peach is rock-hard or mushy, don't buy it.

**Variation:** Most stone fruits are delicious grilled. Try substituting nectarines, plums, or apricots for the peaches.

# Grilled Figs with Honey Mascarpone

*Fresh figs are nothing like those super-sweet cookies we all grew up with. Only available in the summer, these scrumptious fruits are best when simply prepared.*

1 cup mascarpone
1 tablespoon honey, plus extra for garnish
1/2 teaspoon vanilla extract
Vegetable oil, for the grates
8 fresh figs, cut in half lengthwise

2 tablespoons canola oil
1/4 cup finely chopped hazelnuts, optional
  garnish

▶ In a small bowl whisk together the mascarpone, honey, and vanilla. Cover and refrigerate until ready to serve.

▶ Preheat a clean grill to medium-high with the lid closed for 8 to 10 minutes. Lightly brush the grates with oil.

▶ Lightly brush the figs with the canola oil. Place the figs on the grill, cut-side down. Close the grill and cook, turning once, until lightly golden brown, 2 to 3 minutes per side.

▶ To serve, place the figs on a plate. Garnish with a generous spoonful of the mascarpone. Drizzle with honey and chopped hazelnuts if desired.

Serves 4.

**Cooking Tip:** Look for firm, yet ripe, figs. Softer figs could quickly turn mushy when cooked. Enjoy this dish while figs are in season, since dried figs will not work on the grill.

# Strawberry Cake

*This cake is a staple at our summertime family gatherings. Ever since my dad first made it several years ago, it has been a frequently requested favorite. And, luckily, it couldn't be any easier to make. Top a doctored-up box cake mix with fresh whipped cream and just picked strawberries—and voila!—you have a dessert so scrumptious that your guests will be asking for seconds.*

1/3 cup vegetable oil, plus extra to grease
    the pan
All-purpose flour, to flour the pan
1 box (18-ounce) white cake mix
1 cup water
3 eggs

1 1/2 cups strawberry preserves, divided
2 cups heavy cream, chilled
1/4 cup granulated or confectioners' sugar
2 pints strawberries, hulled and halved

▶ Preheat the oven to 350°F. Grease and flour two 9-inch cake pans and set aside.

▶ In the bowl of an electric mixer, combine the white cake mix, water, 1/3 cup oil, eggs, and 1 cup of the strawberry preserves. Beat the mixture until smooth. Pour the batter, dividing it equally, into the prepared cake pans. Bake the cakes until a toothpick inserted in the center comes out clean, 25 to 30 minutes.

▶ Remove the cakes from the oven and cool in the pans on wire racks until cool enough to handle, about 10 minutes. Remove the cakes from the pans and place onto wire racks to cool completely.

▶ In the bowl of an electric mixer, whip the cream and sugar until soft peaks form.

▶ Place one cake layer on a serving plate. Evenly spread 1/4 cup of the remaining preserves over the cake. Then spread half of the whipped cream over the preserves and top with a layer of strawberries. Place the second cake layer on top and evenly spread the remaining 1/4 cup preserves on top. Finish off with a layer each of whipped cream and fresh strawberries. Refrigerate until ready to serve.

Serves 8 to 10.

**Cooking Tip:** Don't need a whole cake? Just garnish one layer and freeze the second layer for another day. It will keep for up to 2 months tightly wrapped in your freezer.

**Do-Ahead:** This cake can be assembled and refrigerated up to 4 hours in advance. If refrigerated longer, it will still be delicious but not as pretty, The whipped cream will start to wilt and soak into the cake layers.

# Many Thanks

Paul, for your unwavering love and support.

My sweet Hannah and Sarah, for being troopers as I experimented on the grill. I promise never ever to grill a strawberry again!

Nevada Presley, for helping me proofread, edit, and test recipes. Your positive attitude, energy, and tireless support helped make writing this book a joy.

Justin Fox Burks, for making this book beautiful with your stunning photography and for being so much fun to work with—even on those 100-degree-plus days when we were melting outside by the grill!

Dad, for sharing your kitchen secrets and your passion for good food.

Mom and Maria, for being the best grandmothers ever and spoiling my girls while I put together this book.

Bob, for pulling out your red pen and helping proofread recipes.

Babcock Gifts, for once again sharing your picture-perfect dishes, linens, and serving pieces. Not only is your collection outstanding, your team is remarkably knowledgeable and delightful.

STOK™ Grills, for use of your fabulous and fun grills. Your grilling inserts and accessories have simplified how I grill. The interchangeable cooking inserts, such as the vegetable tray and the chicken roaster insert, are innovative and take the guesswork out of grilling just about anything!

Lodge Cast Iron, for sharing the grill pans, Dutch ovens, and fajita dishes that allow me to grill inside and out.

To the best group of recipe testers an author could ever ask for: Cindy Ettingoff, Tom Hanemann, Kristen Keegan, Jeri Moskovitz, Amy Pearce, Tommy Prest, Mary Katherine Redd, Brian Schaffler, Macrae Schaffler, Will Sharp, Ginny Strubing, Jenny Vergos, and Patricia Wilson.

To the talented cooks who shared secrets from their kitchens: Lacy Apperson, Justin Fox Burks, Tom Conlee, Tom Hanemann, Beba and Ricardo

Heros, Lucia Heros, Jackson Kramer, Gay Landaiche, Emily Martin, Ernie Mellor, Pete Niedbala, Nevada Presley, Diane Rogol, Susan Rogol, Macrae Schaffler, Will Sharp, Collyn Wainwright, and Ashley Woodman.

To my dear friends who lent me their plates, linens, and serving pieces to use in photos: Amy Barry, Justin Fox Burks, Valerie Dillard, Barbara Hanemann, Maritucker Hanemann, and Melissa Petersen.

To Joel Miller, Heather Skelton, Jason Jones, Kristen Vasgaard, and all the folks at Thomas Nelson Publishers who helped bring this book to life.

To all my Facebook and Twitter friends (I consider you friends not fans!), who shared ideas and suggestions to make this book the best it could be.

# Credits

Many thanks to Babcock Gifts for the use of their dishes and linens in the following photos:

Charred Corn and Black Bean Salsa (page 18)

Grilled Tomato and Vidalia Onion Bruschetta (page 32)

Veggie Stack (page 38)

Tequila Chicken Fajitas (page 52)

Prosciutto and Fontina Stuffed Chicken Breasts (page 56)

Lemon-Oregano Chicken (page 58)

Cowboy T-Bone with Whiskey Butter (page 76)

Honey-Rosemary Pork Chops (page 78)

Pork Souvlaki (page 80)

Blackened Swordfish with Fresh Corn and Tomato Relish (page 102)

Canoe Trout (page 104)

Hoisin-Glazed Sea Bass (page 110)

Honey Mustard Salmon (page 116)

Grouper Tacos with Jalapeno-Lime Slaw (page 118)

Grilled Tuna with Orange and Fennel Slaw (page 120)

Grilled Tilapia with Lemon and Caper Sauce (page 126)

Grilled Halibut with Cherry Tomato Salad (page 132)

Asparagus and Cherry Tomato Salad (page 126)

Cashew Noodle Salad with Miso-Ginger Tofu Skewers (page 132)

Grilled Chicken Salad with Asparagus and Blue Cheese (page 136)

Grilled Shrimp with Cucumber and Heirloom Tomato Salad (page 138)

Tuna Nicoise Salad with Lemon-Caper Vinaigrette (page 140)

Mediterranean Quinoa Salad (page 144)

Grilled Potato Salad (page 148)

Grilled Avocado BLT Salad (page 152)

Tuscan Chicken Sandwich (page 164)

Tuna Burgers with Wasabi Slaw (page 166)

The Ultimate Burger (page 167)

Grilled Salmon Burgers with Dill Tartar Sauce (page 174)

Blackened Snapper Po-Boy (page 176)

Grilled Lime Sweet Potatoes (page 184)

Lemony Grilled Fennel (page 188)

Spinach-Stuffed Portobello Mushrooms (page 192)

Miso Eggplant (page 196)

Grilled Zucchini Ribbons with Fresh Mint and Pine Nuts (page 202)

Grilled Cherry Tomatoes with Sweet Basil Vinaigrette (page 204)

Grilled Radicchio with Balsamic Vinegar and Feta (page 208)

Grilled Polenta Cakes with White Wine Mushrooms (page 210)

Café Au Lait Granita (page 216)

Grilled Peaches and Pound Cake (page 230)

Many thanks to Lodge Cast Iron for the use of their pieces in the following photos:

Charred Corn and Black Bean Salsa (page 18)

Grilled Nachos (page 24)

BBQ Chicken (page 44)

Skirt Steak Fajitas (page 84)

New Orleans–Style Barbecue Shrimp (page 112)

Many thanks to STOK™ Grills for the use of their grills in the following photos:

Grilled Pizza Margarita (page 28)

Beer Can Chicken (page 46)

Grilled Summer Squashes (page 186)

# About the Author

Jennifer Chandler is a wizard in the kitchen with a hint of Southern charm. While she boasts a degree from Le Cordon Bleu, this down-home Mom is about making real food for real families. She's adorable, approachable, and will remind you of the "the girl next door."

When asked why she got into the food business, Jennifer Chandler always quickly responds, "Because I love to eat!" Jennifer's love of good food has led her down an interesting—and tasty—road over the past 15 years.

In 1993, Jennifer surprised everyone when she told them that she was giving up a career in international finance to move to Paris to learn to cook. Jennifer enrolled at the famed Le Cordon Bleu academy, took a crash course in French, and a year later, graduated at the top of her class with *Le Grand Diplome* and a *Mention Tres Bien* in Pastry.

The year she spent in Paris, which included an internship in the pastry shop of Hôtel Plaza Athénée, taught her to appreciate food as something to enjoy and savor. After that life-changing year in Paris, she cut her teeth in the food biz with a stint at a Washington, DC restaurant group, as well as working in the pastry shop at one of the east coast's top caterers. After moving back home to Memphis, Tennessee, Jennifer briefly considered getting a 9-to-5 career, but soon found herself dreaming of the kitchen.

For several years, Jennifer owned a prepared foods market and bakery in Memphis called Cheffie's Market and More. "Our customers loved the convenience of Cheffie's. They could pick up pre-cooked fresh and delicious meals that only needed to be briefly reheated to serve," says Chandler. "Our selection of over fifty items—ranging from salads to side dishes to entrees—was prepared fresh daily by a team of the top chefs in Memphis." Voted "Best New Restaurant in Memphis," Cheffie's received much acclaim and many awards. While the restaurant closed after two years so Jennifer could focus on her expanding family, it has been reincarnated as Cheffie's Café which opened mid-March 2011 to widely anticipated excitement by the entire Memphis community.

With the birth of her second child, Jennifer decided to turn her food career into a more family-friendly one, and because she couldn't leave the business altogether, she started food writing. A contributing writer to several magazines such as *Prevention, Pilates Style, MidSouth, Nashville Home & Garden, Memphis, Edible Memphis, Real Food*, and *Delta*, Jennifer is also a contributing food columnist for *The Commercial Appeal* (a Memphis newspaper).

Jennifer has appeared on numerous broadcast cooking segments including Food Network's "Dinner Impossible," *Better TV*; and she has also been a contributor to Martha Stewart Radio on Sirius/XM. Her motto is: Good Food Simply. Dinnertime can be stress-free and an enjoyable experience for all—even the home chef.

# About the Photographer

Justin Fox Burks was born in Greenwood, Mississippi and raised in Memphis, Tennessee, where he graduated with a B.A. in photography from The University of Memphis. A professional freelance photographer since 1998, he has worked with clients such as M.T.V., the American Lung Association, and Rhodes College; he also shoots for London-based *Mojo* magazine. Justin's food photography has appeared in *Food & Wine*, *Garden & Gun*, and *The London Independent*, as well as the local Dining Out column in *Memphis Magazine* and the *Memphis Flyer*'s weekly Recommended Dish.

Justin's career as a photographer allowed him access to some of the secrets of the South's greatest kitchens, where he picked up tips and tricks from many talented chefs.

Justin is proud to call Memphis home, and he finds a constant source of inspiration from his family, friends, and the characters that inhabit this unique city. Find his photography portfolio online at www.justinfoxburks.com.

He shares the recipes he and his wife Amy Lawrence make in their home kitchen through their blog, The Chubby Vegetarian (www.thechubbyvegetarian.com) and has a forthcoming book, *The Southern Vegetarian Cookbook* (Thomas Nelson Publishing, 2013).

# Index